# 95 Phonics Booster Bundle™

## Summer School Edition

### Rising 2nd Grade

Teacher Edition

Written and published by
95 Percent Group Inc.
Susan L. Hall, EdD, Founder and Chief Executive Officer
475 Half Day Road, Suite 350
Lincolnshire, IL 60069
www.95percentgroup.com

# Table of Contents

## Introduction


Description of *95 Booster Bundle™: Summer School Edition* (SSE) . . . . . . . . . . . . . . . . . . . . . . . . iv

Rationale for Developing the *Summer School Edition* . . . . . . . . . . . . . . . . . . . . . . . . . . . . . iv

How to Use the *Summer School Edition* . . . . . . . . . . . . . . . . . . . . . . . . . . . . . . . . . . . . v

Materials . . . . . . . . . . . . . . . . . . . . . . . . . . . . . . . . . . . . . . . . . . . . . . . . . . . . v

Program Components . . . . . . . . . . . . . . . . . . . . . . . . . . . . . . . . . . . . . . . . . . . . vi

Student Engagement . . . . . . . . . . . . . . . . . . . . . . . . . . . . . . . . . . . . . . . . . . . vii

Alignment with the Science of Reading . . . . . . . . . . . . . . . . . . . . . . . . . . . . . . . . . . vii

Alignment of the *95 Phonics Booster Bundle Summer School Edition* . . . . . . . . . . . . . . . . . . . . x
with 95 Percent Group's Core and Intervention Materials

Scope and Sequence . . . . . . . . . . . . . . . . . . . . . . . . . . . . . . . . . . . . . . . . . . . xi

Overview of Lesson Structure . . . . . . . . . . . . . . . . . . . . . . . . . . . . . . . . . . . . . . . xi

English Learners and Students on IEPs for Reading . . . . . . . . . . . . . . . . . . . . . . . . . . . . xii

Reference List . . . . . . . . . . . . . . . . . . . . . . . . . . . . . . . . . . . . . . . . . . . . . . xiii


## Lessons


**Day 1–5:** Short Vowels a, e, i, o, u . . . . . . . . . . . . . . . . . . . . . . . . . . . . . . . . . . 2

**Day 6–10:** Initial 3-Letter Blends . . . . . . . . . . . . . . . . . . . . . . . . . . . . . . . . . . 30

**Day 11–15:** Consonant Digraphs ch, sh, th, wh . . . . . . . . . . . . . . . . . . . . . . . . . . . . 52

**Day 16–20:** Long Vowel Silent-e . . . . . . . . . . . . . . . . . . . . . . . . . . . . . . . . . . . 82

**Day 21–25:** Closed, Simple Multisyllable . . . . . . . . . . . . . . . . . . . . . . . . . . . . . . 112

# Introduction

### Description of *95 Phonics Booster Bundle™: Summer School Edition* (SSE)

The *95 Phonics Booster Bundle™: Summer School Edition* (SSE) is a phonics strand taught in summer school with the whole class or in small groups. An additional use of the program is to teach part or all of the first 25 days in the fall to jump-start the transition to the next school year. This will help ensure that students have mastered the prior year's skills.

This program is consistent with a core value of 95 Percent Group, which is that reading instruction should be teacher directed. Although digital tools are included, this program is grounded in the belief that the teacher—not a computer—teaches students how to read. The 25 daily lessons in this program are designed to teach for 30–45 minutes daily during summer school or as a review at the beginning of the school year. This program serves as a phonics and word study strand and is not intended to be a comprehensive literacy curriculum; it doesn't include read-alouds, oral language and vocabulary development, reading of authentic text, comprehension instruction, and process writing.

By varying the number of practice opportunities provided to students, teachers can manage the lesson time to 30–45 minutes to fit into a summer school schedule. For example, if less time is available, teachers can dictate 1–2 of the 3 sentences provided for writing or use only 1 of the 2 comprehension questions shown in the Teacher's Edition (TE).

### Rationale for Developing the *Summer School Edition*

Clients have often asked 95 Percent Group to consider developing a Tier 1 phonics program. Across the company's history, this has been the single most requested new product. The impetus for this request is the large, measurable gains occurring among the students receiving instruction with 95 Percent Group's intervention materials. Having experienced what explicit, systematic, and sequential phonics instruction looks like, clients realize that their core program lacks phonics instruction grounded in the science of reading and the principles of structured literacy. Although a handful of clients have successfully used the intervention routines within their core reading block, most clients have experienced challenges adapting our phonics intervention materials for whole-class use.

Based on client feedback, this program addresses the following needs:

- Inadequate phonics instruction in many popular literacy curricula
- An excessive number of students identified for Tier 2 or 3 phonics intervention
- Inadequate teacher knowledge about the science of reading and effective phonics instruction
- Gaps in students' phonics skill development resulting from school closures, summer breaks, etc.
- A curriculum that enables a seamless transition between in-class and remote learning without disrupting or watering down the instruction
- Digital tools to enhance instruction in any setting

Using the deep phonics expertise of our team as well as leveraging instructional strategies found in our existing phonics products, this new *Summer School Edition* phonics program was not only developed quickly but also entirely by our educator employees. A hallmark of the curriculum is that it provides explicit routines in each of the important components of phonics instruction, including word sorting, sound-spelling mapping with and without phonics chips, word chains, and transfer to text. This program aligns with all of 95 Percent Group's phonics assessments and intervention materials so students will have consistent gestures, chip colors, and routines between Tier 1, summer school, and intervention. New decodable text was written so that passages used in our intervention materials will be fresh for students who require extra support in Tier 2 or 3.

Additionally, to address the potential of school closures, the program was designed to ensure a seamless transition to remote learning without disruption in the curriculum sequence by sending the Student Workbook and manipulatives home. These materials can be used from home in unison with the Presentation files when teachers instruct students on videoconferencing platforms.

## How to Use the *Summer School Edition*

Using the *Summer School Edition* is easy because it's an all-inclusive program where teachers receive everything needed for instruction. There is 1 digital component (the Presentation files), which is provided on the company's website at www.95percentgroup.com.

To get started, teachers should read this entire introduction and watch the product training video located online in the Customer Portal (single sign-on). After that, they'll need to cut out the phonics chips and place them in individual student plastic bags (schools will have to provide snack- or sandwich-sized resealable bags for the phonics chips).

A day in the life of a teacher with this program means simply reviewing the lesson ahead of time. Just before instruction begins, teachers turn to the starting page in the TE and display, on a screen, the header page in the Presentation file for that day's lesson. After instructing students to retrieve their individual chip bags and workbooks, the teacher spends 30–45 minutes going back and forth between drawing the students' attention to the screen and giving them time to work in their workbooks. Students sort words, map sounds in boxes, underline pattern words, read a passage, and respond to the passages through oral and written prompts.

## Materials

There are 2 types of materials included in the Rising 2nd Grade SSE program: printed teacher and student materials, and presentation files accessed online at the product's Customer Portal.

### Printed Materials Shipped

- **Teacher's Package** – The Teacher's Package includes 1 full-color, spiral-bound TE for Rising 2nd grade. Each TE includes 25 days of lessons. The back cover is a firm stock, enabling teachers to hold the book folded back to see a single page with assurance that it will not bend. The other printed component is a set of Sound-Spelling Cards the teacher holds up while introducing and reviewing the phonics concepts. These cards are included in the shrink-wrapping surrounding the TE.

- **Student Package** – The Student Package includes 2 components. First, there is a Student Workbook (SW) of approximately 46 pages with full-color covers and grayscale printing on the interior pages. The workbook includes copies of passages that students can write on, word lists and columns for sorting words by pattern, boxes for word mapping, tables for completing word chains from teacher dictation, and designated areas to write responses to passage comprehension questions. The second component is the student manipulatives, which include a sound-spelling mat and a sheet of chips that provide the student with an individual set of manipulatives to use during the lessons. The manipulatives are printed in color on a larger sheet that is pulled out from the center of the SW binding. One half of the paper is the sound-spelling mat and the other half contains rectangle chips (for silent-e instruction) and circle chips. Teachers will need to cut out the chips for storage in snack- or sandwich-sized resealable bags (provided by schools).

### Materials Accessed Online at the Customer Portal

- **Presentation Files** – These HTML animated files contain images to guide instruction of the lessons. Teachers access and use the Presentation files on our website either in the classroom or during remote instruction using a videoconferencing platform such as Zoom or Google® Classroom. Because these files are HTML, they are accessible on any device with a current browser, including a Chromebook®.
- **Product Training Video** – This 30-minute training video provides an overview of the program and tips for teaching the lessons. This video is accessible on the Customer Portal by all teachers who have a Teacher's Package. More extensive professional development is available either virtually or in person for an additional fee.
- **Other Teacher Support** – The product's landing page will be updated with teacher support tips and resources as new questions arise. Teachers should check back frequently for additional resources.

## Program Components

The *Summer School Edition* is a phonics curriculum that is designed for rising K-2nd grade students and includes the following components:

- Phonological awareness instruction and practice to develop and support phonemic proficiency for efficient word recognition skills
- Letter-sound correspondences
- Letter formation instruction and practice
- Suggestions for developing print concepts while reading text aloud
- Explicit instruction in blending CVC words
- Phonics patterns that are demonstrated and practiced hands-on with phonics chips
- Phoneme-grapheme mapping, including writing letters in sound boxes in the Student Workbook
- High-frequency word practice (based on the Dolch grade-level list)
- Writing words, word chains, sentences, and short responses to passage reading
- Word and phrase fluency practice
- Practice applying phonics knowledge in decodable text specifically written to provide maximum practice for pattern words and to review previously taught patterns

 

- Instruction in morphological units, including derivational and inflectional suffixes, the most common prefixes and suffixes (based on the work of Marcia K. Henry, author of *Unlocking Literacy* and a consultant to 95 Percent Group in the design of our vocabulary product, *Vocabulary Surge*)
- Instruction and practice in the use of standards-based comprehension processes through oral discussions and written responses after students read decodable texts

## Student Engagement

Student engagement is critically important for learning. Stanislas Dehaene's books *Reading in the Brain* and *How We Learn* provide research on the importance of not only holding students' attention but also helping to direct their attention to what's important to learn. He states in *How We Learn* (2020) that research in cognitive science shows that attention is the mechanism used by the brain to select information, amplify it, channel it, and deepen the processing of it. He reports on research that shows that whatever the learner pays attention to causes a strong surge of neural firings, exactly what the synapses need to change their strength and cause learning to happen. In the *95 Phonics Core Summer School Edition*, multiple techniques are used—such as pointing a finger at vowels in the phonics pattern—to focus the learner's attention on what matters.

In the lesson design of the *Summer School Edition*, there are many techniques to not only engage students but also to focus their attention on key visual information that will facilitate automaticity in the recognition and reading of phonics patterns. It's not possible to learn words individually because there are too many in the English language. The approach in the *Summer School Edition* is to teach the pattern, enabling students to generalize to other words with the same pattern.

Here are some of the ways that the instructional routines in the *Summer School Edition* engage and guide students' attention to what is important to learn:

- Finding the vowels by pointing to them
- Using gestures (V-shape, closed fist, open fist, etc.) for syllable types so all students are responding during whole-class instruction
- Using hands-on phonics chip movement to amplify learning phonemic awareness to an automatic level
- Writing words in a word chain to see the difference in spellings (e.g., rip, ripe, ride, rid)
- Analyzing how words change meaning by writing the prefixes in small boxes surrounding the Latin root or Anglo-Saxon base word

Each lesson includes student engagement because it's not only critical for learning but also provides the opportunity for corrective feedback.

## Alignment with the Science of Reading

The *Summer School Edition* is **research based**. It was developed using the same research base that provided the foundation for *Phonics Lesson Library™* and *Phonics Chip Kits™*, developed by 95 Percent Group in 2014–2016 and 2012 respectively. The studies included in the National Reading Panel report were the initial basis of the design for the *Summer School Edition*, which was confirmed by more recent research studies cited in David Kilpatrick's 2015 book, *Essentials of Assessing, Preventing, and Overcoming Reading Difficulties*. Several fundamental research findings that 95 Percent Group used as guiding principles are shown on the next page.

- Phonics instruction that is <u>systematic</u> is better than no preplanned order of skill instruction.
- Effective phonics instruction follows a <u>prescribed sequence</u> that progresses from simple to complex. Our phonics products follow a skills progression that is defined by 95 Percent Group's phonics continuum so that each lesson builds on earlier mastered concepts.
- Explicit instruction produces the best results. 95 Percent Group's phonics products use an explicit approach where students are directly told the phonics concept. The phonics pattern is emphasized and made more explicit in several ways:
  - By using manipulatives (colored chips)
  - By using gestures for the syllable types
  - By reinforcing learning with the reading-writing connection through word chaining, writing words in sound boxes, and writing sentences from dictation
- <u>Orthographic mapping</u> is the process the brain uses to recognize words that are stored in memory. The program supports the importance of orthographic mapping to word learning in several places. First, students identify individual phonemes by moving color-coded sound chips into sound boxes (called Elkonin boxes). Next, our product directs students' attention to the sound-spelling patterns through color-coded sound chips. After mapping the sounds in words, students write letters below, which is the phoneme-grapheme mapping process. David Kilpatrick's book *Essentials of Assessing, Preventing, and Overcoming Reading Difficulties* was released in 2015; the research cited is what was used in the design of the *Summer School Edition*.

Specific, cited research that supports our product design includes:

- *Report of the National Reading Panel: Teaching Children to Read. Report of Subgroups* (2001).
  - "Findings provided solid support for the conclusion that <u>systematic phonics instruction makes a more significant contribution to children's growth in reading than do alternative programs providing unsystematic or no phonics instruction</u>" (p. 2-132).
  - "Phonics instruction has also been <u>widely regarded as particularly beneficial</u> to children with reading problems (e.g., Foorman et al., 1998)" (p. 2-105).
- *Report of the National Reading Panel: Teaching Children to Read Summary Report* (2002).
  - "The meta-analysis revealed that <u>systematic phonics instruction</u> produces significant benefits for students in kindergarten through 6th grade and for children having difficulty learning to read" (p. 9).
  - "First graders who were taught phonics systematically were better able to decode and spell, and they showed significant improvement in their ability to comprehend text" (p. 9).
  - "Across all grade levels, systematic phonics instruction improved the ability of good readers to spell" (p. 10).
- Kilpatrick, D. (2015). *Essentials of Assessing, Preventing, and Overcoming Reading Difficulties*.
  - "<u>Systematic instruction</u> means that the teacher has a specific plan or sequence for introducing letter-sound relationships" (p. 268).
  - "Because the <u>explicit and systematic approach</u> is more successful with most students, the terms *explicit* and *systematic* are often used to distinguish more effective approaches to phonics instruction from less effective ones" (p. 268).

- "Orthographic memory involves a connection-forming process in which the oral phonemes are 'bonded' to the letters used to represent those phonemes. The phoneme sequence of the word is already established in long-term memory and acts as the anchor for the written sequence of letters used to represent that phonemic sequence" (p. 101).
- "Orthographic mapping establishes a stable memory of spelling patterns" (p. 81).

In regards to **evidence based**, the *Summer School Edition* has not been the subject of an efficacy study because it is new. However, there are two considerations. First, 95 Percent Group plans to conduct an evidence study upon the program's release. Second, the phonics products upon which the *Summer School Edition* is based have been studied and evaluated in evidence studies—and there is much evidence of their success. For more information, please visit our product landing page, which will be updated once evidence studies are completed.

A discussion about the important components of a phonics program is outlined below.

### Phonological Awareness (PA)

Because of the importance of PA in learning to read, the *Summer School Edition* includes a short warm-up of PA at the start of each lesson. As the lessons progress, the PA prompts, which contain advanced phonemic manipulation skills, increase in complexity from adding, deleting, and substituting initial and final sounds to substituting a sound in a consonant blend and complex vowel substitutions.

### Orthographic Mapping

One of the most important new insights from the past 5 years is that instructing students to study letter strings is more effective than using cues such as context or initial letter to figure out an unknown word. The process of going from speech to print is critical in developing an image of the letter strings in a word. The *Summer School Edition* explicitly teaches the link between the phonemic sounds in a word and the letter or letters that spell each sound. 95 Percent Group developed an approach where specific colored chips represent certain types of sounds; this approach was published in 2012 as the *Phonics Chip Kit* and more recently incorporated in the 2020 *95 Phonics Core Program*™. The recent attention to the process of orthographic mapping—mapping letters to sounds—confirms our approach of emphasizing sound-spelling mapping. The *Summer School Edition* includes sound-spelling mapping with and without chips in many of the days.

### Fluency

Fluency occurs when the reader recognizes nearly all the words in a text. According to Joseph Torgeson (2004), readers achieve fluency when they not only have a sufficient Word Bank of known words but also have the skills to efficiently figure out new words.

To prepare students to fluently read connected text, it's best to support gradual steps to getting there. First, they need fluency at the word level. Then, they need to read phrases. Finally, fluency occurs at the sentence and paragraph levels.

### High-Frequency Words (HFWs)

The *Summer School Edition* uses the Dolch list of high-frequency words for kindergarten through grade 2. Students are exposed to the words in the passages and get a chance to increase their automatic recognition of the words through daily fluency practice reading the words. Most of the words become decodable once the skill is taught in the program. For example, the word *must* is included in Dolch's grade K list. The closed syllable pattern with consonant digraph *th* is taught in Days 11–15 of the Rising 2nd lessons; after that, the word *with* is no longer considered a HFW because it is now decodable by the pattern that has been taught.

**Passage Reading**

The *Summer School Edition*'s Rising 2nd-grade curriculum includes 10 passages. The program includes 5 informational passages and 5 literary passages, which are important for developing skills related to the Common Core standards.

The writers at 95 Percent Group are all educators and intimately familiar with the skill sequence we use not only in the *Summer School Edition* but also in the *Phonics Lesson Library* and the *95 Phonics Core Program*. The writers are not professionally hired external writers—they are the same educators who provide professional development for our phonics products. They know the sequence and appreciate how carefully designed these passages are for student success.

Each passage is written to have a significant percentage of pattern words; the purpose of using decodable text is to provide students, who have just reviewed and practiced reading words with a specific phonics pattern with sufficient practice applying their knowledge to reading words in connected text. Before writing any passages, our design team established guidelines that specified several things. First, a percentage of pattern words to include in a passage based on the level of utility of the phonics pattern. The passages vary in length from approximately 150–300 words for Rising 2nd and Rising 3rd-grade. Each passage completed a review process through four reviewers who not only offered suggested improvements but also checked that no words above the phonics sequence were used, excluding allowable high-frequency words as defined on the Dolch list.

95 Percent Group developed a process called "Transfer to Text." It provides a structured approach to helping students recognize pattern words in a text so their knowledge of how to read the phonics pattern will be activated when reading the words within a longer text. This process has been highly regarded and is used with permission in *Language Essentials for Teachers of Reading and Spelling* (LETRS) and the Texas Education Department's reading academies.

## Alignment of the *95 Phonics Booster Bundle Summer School Edition* with 95 Percent Group's Core and Intervention Materials

The compatibility of 95 Percent Group's summer school phonics program with our newly created core and well-established interventions is seamless. The *Summer School Edition* is intentionally designed to align with all our other phonics products in the following ways:

- All our phonics products (*Phonics Lesson Library*, *Phonics Chip Kits*, and *95 Phonics Core Program*™) are aligned to the same phonics continuum and the same scope and sequence.
- Because the skills in the *Summer School Edition* are taught in the same sequence as our intervention programs, placement in intervention is straightforward. If a student doesn't master a skill with Tier 1 instruction, the teacher will know immediately where to start intervention in Tier 2 or 3.
- The phonics chip colors are the same in core, summer school, and small-group intervention instruction; it is preferable for students who struggle not to switch colors or approaches between what they hear in whole-class and small-group instruction.
- The syllable gestures are the same between Tier 1 and intervention (e.g., closed fist for closed syllables, V-shaped fingers for the silent-e syllable, etc.).

- The key instructional routines are taught the same way in Tier 1 and intervention (for example, in a word chain, the students are asked which sound changes before being asked which letter changes). Students will have learned the routines in the *Summer School Edition* and this should accelerate progress in small-group interventions.
- The decodable text for the *Summer School Edition* has been written specifically for each lesson; therefore students who need intervention will be exposed to text that is new to them, so they won't have memorized it and must use their pattern-recognition skills to read unfamiliar words.

When schools use different Tier 1 and intervention programs, struggling students often fail to generalize and transfer skills because of misalignment in instructional practices between the programs. Students spend too much attention trying to switch back and forth in routines, colors, procedures, and techniques as they transition from Tier 1 to intervention. By using a summer school program with the same structured literacy processes as the 95 Percent Group core and intervention materials, students who receive instruction in summer school benefit from the crossover of processes, strategies, and instructional language. In fact, implementing a strong, comprehensive summer school phonics program that is explicit, sequential, and cumulative should reduce the need for intervention for a percentage of students during the traditional school year.

## Scope and Sequence

The scope and sequence for the *Summer School Edition* is available for download on the product's landing page in the Customer Portal.

## Overview of Lesson Structure

The Rising 2nd lessons include the following sections in all lessons (see the detailed scope and sequence on the Customer Portal):

- **Phonological Awareness Warm-Up** – Each day starts with a warm-up.
- **Phonics Pattern** – There is a 5-day instructional cycle for teaching phonics patterns. The pattern is explicitly taught on the first day, is reviewed on the second day, and is applied on the 3 days following that.
- **Sound-Spelling Mapping (with and without chips)** – Students have multiple opportunities in the lessons to map words that the teacher dictates. Some days mapping is done with chips, and other days students move from finger-stretching to writing letters in boxes.
- **Fluency** – Within the cycle of teaching a phonics pattern, students practice at the word and phrase levels with 1-minute timed readings. Fluency grids with both high-frequency and pattern words are included.
- **Sentence Dictation** – Students write sentences the teacher dictates and then correct them by looking at a correct version. Punctuation is emphasized.
- **Passages** – Text reading is included within the 5-day instructional cycle for a phonics pattern. On Days 1 and 3, students identify pattern words by underlining them in the passage. On Days 2 and 4, they read the underlined words and then the entire passage. On Day 5, students read both passages.
- **Comprehension** – Within the 5-day instructional cycle for a phonics pattern, on Days 2, 4, and 5, students provide either oral or written responses to the text; the comprehension questions are labeled in the TE by Common Core reading standard.

 95 Phonics Booster Bundle™: Summer School Edition 2021 • Rising Second • Teacher's Edition **xi**

# English Learners and Students on IEPs for Reading

## English Learners

English Learners (ELs) often need instruction in the phonological structure of a new language, especially when those structures differ from their native language. For example, Spanish-speaking students often need support to help them move from the syllabic structure of their native language to the phonemic structure of English. This instruction can be good for all English Learners. Those with strength in the phonological structure of their native language will pick up the new language fairly quickly with some instruction. Those with a deficit in their native language will require more explicit instruction. Clients have provided evidence to us that their ELs benefit from and make excellent progress with our materials because the instructional routines provide explicit information about the structure of the English language. Additionally, the embedded routines allow students to move through advanced levels more quickly, preparing them for higher levels of orthographic mapping.

## Students on IEPs for Reading Disabilities

Through the continuous teacher–student interaction of the gradual release model, teachers are able to differentiate and scaffold as necessary. This allows teachers to spend as much—or as little—time as necessary on a given skill. Moving students forward as quickly as we can, but as slowly as we must, is key to effective intervention instruction.

In order to provide differentiated instruction for students who are struggling, all of the lessons in the *Summer School Edition*, as well as in the *Phonics Lesson Library, Phonics Chip Kit*, and *95 Phonics Core Program*, have the I DO, WE DO, YOU DO modeling cycle. This cycle provides a gradual release from teacher modeling to students successfully doing the task independently.

All the phonics programs from 95 Percent Group, including the *Summer School Edition*, use manipulatives in instruction. Manipulatives are useful, especially in providing support for students who struggle to learn the skills. All the senses are used in these multisensory lessons. Some examples are:

- Visual – Students see the letters.
- Auditory – Students hear the teacher segmenting the words into individual sounds.
- Kinesthetic – Students make gestures and move their pencils when writing letters in the sound boxes.
- Tactile – Students feel the pencil as they write on paper.

During the I DO and WE DO portions of the lesson, the visual and auditory sensory pathways of students are engaged simultaneously though teacher modeling and presentation with manipulatives such as sound chips, Elkonin boxes, word cards, and decodable texts. The WE DO portion of the lesson engages visual, auditory, and kinesthetic senses.

  

## Reference List


- Dehaene, S. (2017). Reading in the brain: The science and evolution of a human invention. New York, NY: Viking.
- Dehaene, S. (2020). How we learn: Why brains learn better than any machine…for now. New York, NY: Viking.
- Dolch Word. (n.d.). Dolch word list by grade (frequency). http://www.dolchword.net/dolch-word-list-frequency-grade.html
- Eunice Kennedy Shriver National Institute of Child Health and Human Development, NIH, DHHS. (2000). Report of the National Reading Panel: Teaching children to read: Reports of the subgroups (00-4754). Washington, DC: U.S. Government Printing Office.
- Farrell, L., Hunter, M., & Osenga, T. (2019). A new model for teaching high-frequency words. WETA Reading Rockets. https://www.readingrockets.org/article/new-model-teaching-high-frequency-words. Downloaded 6-8-2020.
- Henry, M. (2010). Unlocking literacy: Effective decoding & spelling instruction (2nd ed.). Baltimore, MD: Paul H. Brookes.
- Kilpatrick, D. A. (2015). Essentials of assessing, preventing, and overcoming reading difficulties. Hoboken, NJ: John Wiley & Sons.
- Kilpatrick, D. A. (2016). Equipped for reading success: A comprehensive, step by step program for developing phonemic awareness and fluent word recognition. Syracuse, NY: Casey & Kirsch Publishers.
- *Seidenberg, M. (2017). Language at the speed of sight: How we read, why so many can't, and what can be done about it. New York, NY: Basic Books.*
- Torgesen, J. K. (2004). Avoiding the devastating downward spiral: The evidence that early intervention prevents reading failure. American Educator, 28(3), 6–19.
- WISE Channel. (2013, October 25). How the brain learns to read - Prof. Stanislas Dehaene [Video file]. Retrieved from https://www.youtube.com/watch?v=25GI3-kiLdo


 

# Gus and Peg

1  I have two pet cats who like catnip. Gus is my little cat, and
2  Peg is my big cat. When I got Peg, she was a little kitten. She was
3  little like Gus. Now Peg is a big cat.
4  Gus and Peg like to play. Gus likes to hop and run. Peg
5  likes to run and dig. The vet said that Gus and Peg are fit.
6  I got catnip for my cats. Peg and Gus like catnip. When
7  Peg sees the catnip bag, she runs to get it. She bats the bag
8  with her legs. Gus likes to get the catnip too. I put the bag on
9  the bed. They hop on top of the bed on my laptop to get the
10  catnip bag.
11  Gus and Peg like to play. Gus and Peg have fun. I can
12  help Gus and Peg get fit. I can help my cats hop and run.

**Note:** The words *little, when, was, now, play, that, for, with, her, they,* and *help* are not considered pattern words. The high-frequency words *when, that, with, they,* and *help* will not be considered pattern words until consonant blends and digraphs are reviewed in Days 6–15. The word *little* is a 2-syllable high-frequency word. The remaining high-frequency words listed above are not pronounced with a short vowel sound.

| Single Syllable, Short Vowels | | | | | Multisyllable |
| --- | --- | --- | --- | --- | --- |
| Short a | Short e | Short i | Short o | Short u | Closed-Closed |
| and | bed | big | got | fun | catnip |
| bag | leg | dig | hop | Gus | kitten |
| bat | Peg | fit | on | run | laptop |
| can | pet | is | top | up | |
| cat | vet | it | | | |

| Word Count* |
| --- |
| 154 |
| **Pattern Words** |
| 87 (56%) |

* including title

**Passage – Informational**

# The [Canyon]

1     I get to go to a big [canyon] with my sis, Val. The [canyon] is

2 set down a bit. You can [zigzag] to get down. If you look up, you

3 can see the big tops. There is blue fog on the rim at the top.

4 When we sit in the [canyon,] the men on top look as little as dots.

5     We go up to the rim that sits at the [canyon] tip. A bus

6 can zip you up to the tip top of the rim. If you get to the top at

7 [sunset,] the [canyon] looks pretty. It is red and yellow down in the

8 big pit. When the [sunset] is under the rim, it is dim in the [canyon.]

9     If you go to a [canyon,] one tip is to get to the top when

10 the sun sets. It is pretty and can be lots of fun!

**Note:** The words *with*, *down*, *when*, *little*, *that*, *pretty*, *yellow*, and *under* are not considered pattern words. The high-frequency words *with*, *when*, and *that* will not be considered pattern words until consonant digraphs are reviewed in Days 11–15. The words *little*, *under*, *pretty*, and *yellow* are 2-syllable high-frequency words. The word *down* has the vowel team *ow* and is not pronounced with a short vowel sound.

| Single Syllable, Short Vowels | | | | | | Multisyllable |
| Short a | Short e | Short i | | Short o | Short u | Closed-Closed |
|---|---|---|---|---|---|---|
| and | get | big | pit | dot | bus | canyon |
| as | men | bit | rim | fog | fun | sunset |
| at | red | dim | sis | got | sun | zigzag |
| can | set | if | tip | lot | up | |
| | | is | zip | top | | |
| | | it | | | | |

| Word Count* |
|---|
| 149 |
| **Pattern Words** |
| 81 (54%) |

* including title

**Day 1**

# Days 1–5: Short Vowels a, e, i, o, u

## Learning Objective

In Days 1–5, students demonstrate understanding of all short vowel, closed syllables by correctly identifying, reading, and writing pattern words in isolation and in passages. Also, students demonstrate an early understanding of inflected ending -*ed* and simple closed-closed multisyllable words.

## DAY 1

### Phonological Awareness Warm-Up

**Today we are going to practice <u>segmenting all the sounds</u> in a word.**

**Let's practice.**
**Say nap: (nap) Finger-stretch and say the sounds in the word** *nap*. **/n/ /ă/ /p/**
**Say rose: (rose) Sounds? /r/ /ō/ /z/**

**Now it's your turn. Here are the instructions:**
- **I'll say a word and you repeat it.**
- **Then, tell me the sounds in the word. Ready?**

| | | | |
|---|---|---|---|
| Say mat: (mat) Sounds? | /m/ /ă/ /t/ | Say play: (play) Sounds? | /p/ /l/ /ā/ |
| Say sock: (sock) Sounds? | /s/ /ŏ/ /k/ | Say make: (make) Sounds? | /m/ /ā/ /k/ |
| Say kit: (kit) Sounds? | /k/ /ĭ/ /t/ | Say bike: (bike) Sounds? | /b/ /ī/ /k/ |
| Say hat: (hat) Sounds? | /h/ /ă/ /t/ | Say late: (late) Sounds? | /l/ /ā/ /t/ |
| Say pig: (pig) Sounds? | /p/ /ĭ/ /g/ | Say line: (line) Sounds? | /l/ /ī/ /n/ |
| Say light: (light) Sounds? | /l/ /ī/ /t/ | Say bake: (bake) Sounds? | /b/ /ā/ /k/ |
| Say soap: (soap) Sounds? | /s/ /ō/ /p/ | Say kite: (kite) Sounds? | /k/ /ī/ /t/ |
| Say bite: (bite) Sounds? | /b/ /ī/ /t/ | Say seat: (seat) Sounds? | /s/ /ē/ /t/ |

### Phonics Pattern

**Today we are reviewing words with short vowels a, e, i, o, and u. The words follow the closed syllable pattern. A closed syllable has 1 vowel letter followed by 1 or more consonants, the vowel sound is short. It is a closed syllable.**

**The gesture for the closed syllable is a closed fist.**

**Practice the gesture with me.**  **closed**

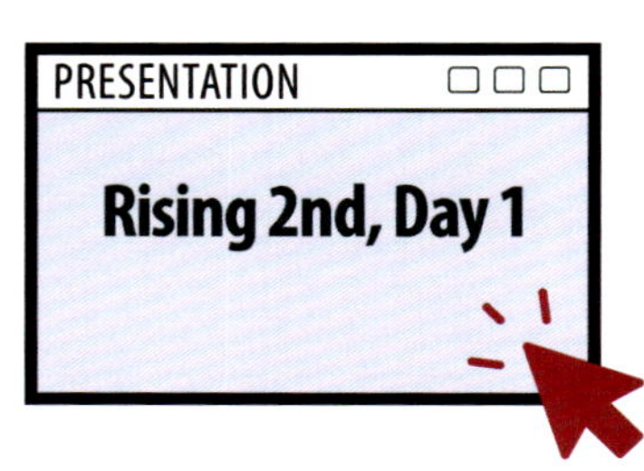

**Repeat it with me:** Closed syllable words have 1 vowel letter (hold pointer finger up) followed by 1 or more consonants (scoop with finger), and the vowel sound is short.  (closed fist gesture)

Let's review the short vowel sounds found in closed syllables. As I show you each Sound-Spelling Card, I will say the vowel sound and keyword, and show the closed gesture. Then, I will ask you to repeat the vowel sound and keyword with me.
- The short sound for the vowel *a* is /ă/. The keyword is apple. Say the sound and keyword with me. /ă/ apple
- The short sound for the vowel *e* is /ĕ/. The keyword is echo. Sound and keyword? /ĕ/ echo
- The short sound for the vowel *i* is /ĭ/. The keyword is itch. Sound and keyword? /ĭ/ itch
- The short sound for the vowel *o* is /ŏ/. The keyword is octopus. Sound and keyword? /ŏ/ octopus
- The short sound for the vowel *u* is /ŭ/. The keyword is up. Sound and keyword? /ŭ/ up

**Note:** Display the Sound-Spelling Cards for the short vowels so the students have a visual cue to reference throughout Days 1–5.

## SORT WORDS

(Display <u>pot</u>.)

**I'm going to look for words with a short vowel sound. Watch the steps I use:**
1. **I find the vowel letter by pointing to it. There is 1 vowel letter. Next, I look to see if there is at least 1 consonant after the vowel. There is 1 vowel letter *o* followed by 1 consonant.**
2. **This word HAS the short o closed pattern. The vowel sound is /ŏ/.**
3. **The gesture looks like this.** 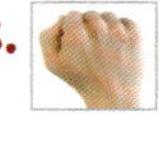 (Gesture and say "closed.")
4. **I place the word in the /ŏ/ octopus column.**  (Don't read the word yet.)

Let's sort the next word together. I'll answer and gesture with you.

(Display <u>nut</u>.)

- **Look at this word. What do I do first?** find the vowel letter
  - Yes, let's pretend to touch the vowel letter.
- **How many vowel letters?** 1
- **Is it followed by 1 or more consonants?** yes
- **Syllable type?** 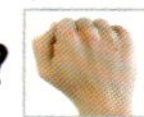 closed
- **Vowel sound?** /ŭ/
- **Where does this word go?**  in the /ŭ/ up column

**Day 1**

| ă | ĕ | ĭ | ŏ | ŭ |
|---|---|---|---|---|
| | | | pot | nut |

 Now it's your turn. Turn to page 2 in your Student Workbook. Identify the short vowel sound in each word. Then, write the word in the correct column. Finally, read all the words in each column.

**Answer Key**

| ă | ĕ | ĭ | ŏ | ŭ |
|---|---|---|---|---|
| pat | pet | pit | pot | nut |
| bag | beg | big | dot | bug |
| fan | | fin | cob | fun |



- **Find the vowels.**
- **How many vowel letters?**
- **Is it followed by 1 or more consonants?**
- **Syllable type and gesture?**
- **Vowel sound?**
- **Where does this word go?**
- **Read the words.**

| | |
|---|---|
| 1. pat | 7. bag |
| 2. pit | 8. big |
| 3. pet | 9. cob |
| 4. beg | 10. fin |
| 5. dot | 11. fan |
| 6. bug | 12. fun |

## Writing

### WORD BUILDING

Now, we will build words using the short vowel sounds.

Watch the steps I use:

- In the first row, I write the letter *a* on the line between the p and t.
- I gesture and say the syllable type:  closed.
- I point to the vowel letter while saying the sound: /ă/.
- Finally, I slide my finger under the word and whisper "pat."

Now it's your turn. Turn to page 2 in your Student Workbook.

1. **Write the vowel between the two consonants.**
2. **Gesture and say the syllable type.**
3. **Point to and whisper the vowel sound.**
4. **Slide your finger under the word as you whisper read it.**

*Note:* The final word *put* in the word building table is not pronounced with the typical short u sound. Allow the students to experiment with the vowel sound before explicitly explaining the word is a high-frequency word and does not follow the expected sound of other short u words. To give students an opportunity to decode typical short u words, write the words *cut, hut,* and *nut* on the board and have the students read them with you.

| Vowels | Word |
|---|---|
| a | p<u>a</u>t |

**Answer Key**

| Vowels | Words |
|---|---|
| a | p<u>a</u>t |
| e | p<u>e</u>t |
| i | p<u>i</u>t |
| o | p<u>o</u>t |
| u | p<u>u</u>t |

## Writing

### WORD COMPLETION WITH PICTURES

Now we're going to complete some words. Look at each picture. Fill in the correct sounds to complete the word. After you write the word, whisper read it.

I'll do the first one. This picture is <u>bed</u>.
- I finger-stretch bed. /b/ /ĕ/ /d/
- I tap the letters and line, while saying the sounds to see what sound is missing. (Tap the letter *b*, the line, and the letter *d*.)
  - The middle sound /ĕ/ is missing. The sound /ĕ/ is spelled with the letter *e*.
- Next, I write the letter *e* in the middle space.
- Finally, I slide my finger under the word and whisper "bed."

 Turn to page 3 in your Student Workbook. Here are the steps:

1. Finger-stretch the sounds.
2. Tap the letters and line while saying the sounds.
3. Write the letter for the missing sound.
4. Whisper read the word.

b <u>e</u> d

### Answer Key

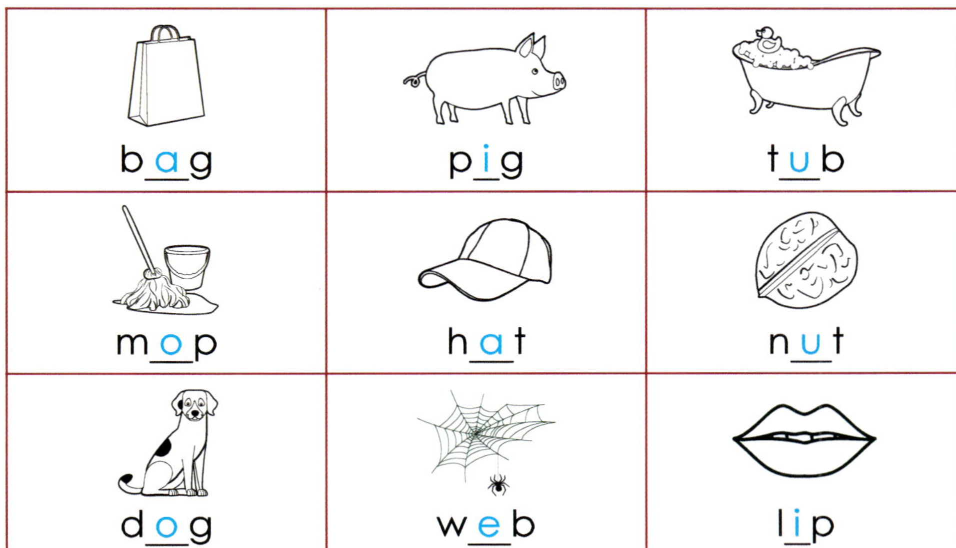

| | | |
|---|---|---|
| b <u>a</u> g | p <u>i</u> g | t <u>u</u> b |
| m <u>o</u> p | h <u>a</u> t | n <u>u</u> t |
| d <u>o</u> g | w <u>e</u> b | l <u>i</u> p |

## Passage Reading

### UNDERLINE/CIRCLE PATTERN WORDS

**Passage – Literary: *Gus and Peg***

**Now we'll practice finding closed syllable words in a passage including a few 2-syllable words. Our passage today is about a kid and 2 pet cats.**

**We are going to look for and underline 1-syllable words containing the closed syllable pattern. We will also look for 2-syllable words with 2 closed syllables and circle them. Then we will sort them in a chart.**

**Let's look at the title of the passage.** (Do not read the title.) **The word *Gus* has 1 vowel, *u*, and is followed by 1 consonant. This word follows the closed syllable pattern, so I make the closed gesture and underline the word. Help me find more words to underline. Hold up the closed syllable gesture when you see another one, and I'll underline it.** (Continue underlining 1-syllable words that follow the closed pattern above the black line.)

**Now, we are going to look for 2-syllable words and circle them. First, I will show you how to read one when you find it. Look at this word.** (Point to catnip.) **I find the vowels and point under them. There are 2 syllables, *cat* and *nip*. You know how to read each syllable; put them together to read the word. Since the word *catnip* has 2 closed syllables, I will circle it.** (Continue this process with the word *kitten*. Stop at the black line.)

**Now that we have underlined and circled the closed syllable words above the black line, we will sort a few of these words together into the table below the passage.**

**The first word we underlined is Gus. It has the short u vowel sound, so I write it in the /ŭ/ up column.**

**I will also sort 1 of the 2-syllable words we found. I will write the word *catnip* in the 2-syllable words column.**

**Now it's your turn. Turn to page 4 in your Student Workbook. Here are the steps:**

1. **Begin at the black line and continue to the end of the passage.**
2. **Use your fingers to find the vowel or vowels.**
3. **If you find a word with the closed syllable pattern, underline it. If you find a multisyllable word with 2 closed syllables, circle it.**
4. **Choose words you underlined and write them in the correct short vowel column. You will only need 2 for each column.**
5. **Complete the last column with one more 2-syllable word you circled.**
6. **Finally, whisper read the words you underlined or circled.**

(Refer to the note under the passage on page 2 for exceptions.)

*Note:* Students may want you to circle the high-frequency word *little* in the passage. Although it is a 2-syllable word, remind the students they are only circling 2-syllable words in which both syllables are closed. The word *little* does not follow this pattern.

| ă  | ĕ | ĭ | ŏ | ŭ | 2-syllable words |
|---|---|---|---|---|---|
| | | | | Gus | catnip |
| | | | | | |

***Note:*** When you call on students to read a word they wrote in their table, ask which column they listed it in. Use the word table below the passage on page 2 to check the answers that students provide.

## DAY 2

### Phonological Awareness Warm-Up

**Today we are going to practice <u>phoneme segmentation</u>. Let's review the instructions:**
- **I'll say a word and you repeat it.**
- **Then, tell me the sounds in the word. Ready?**

| | | | |
|---|---|---|---|
| Say phone: (**phone**) Sounds? | /f/ /ō/ /n/ | Say black: (**black**) Sounds? | /b/ /l/ /ă/ /k/ |
| Say hog: (**hog**) Sounds? | /h/ /ŏ/ /g/ | Say house: (**house**) Sounds? | /h/ /ou/ /s/ |
| Say cut: (**cut**) Sounds? | /k/ /ŭ/ /t/ | Say shell: (**shell**) Sounds? | /sh/ /ĕ/ /l/ |
| Say rake: (**rake**) Sounds? | /r/ /ā/ /k/ | Say slip: (**slip**) Sounds? | /s/ /l/ /ĭ/ /p/ |
| Say sit: (**sit**) Sounds? | /s/ /ĭ/ /t/ | Say fly: (**fly**) Sounds? | /f/ /l/ /ī/ |
| Say tag: (**tag**) Sounds? | /t/ /ă/ /g/ | Say help: (**help**) Sounds? | /h/ /ĕ/ /l/ /p/ |
| Say plate: (**plate**) Sounds? | /p/ /l/ /ā/ /t/ | Say rag: (**rag**) Sounds? | /r/ /ă/ /g/ |
| Say flip: (**flip**) Sounds? | /f/ /l/ /ĭ/ /p/ | Say clock: (**clock**) Sounds? | /k/ /l/ /ŏ/ /k/ |

### Phonics Pattern

#### READING PATTERN WORDS

**Review the Pattern**

We're continuing to read and spell words with the closed syllable pattern.

**Repeat after me:** Closed syllable words have 1 vowel letter followed by 1 or more consonants, and the vowel sound is short.

**Gesture and say the syllable type.**  closed

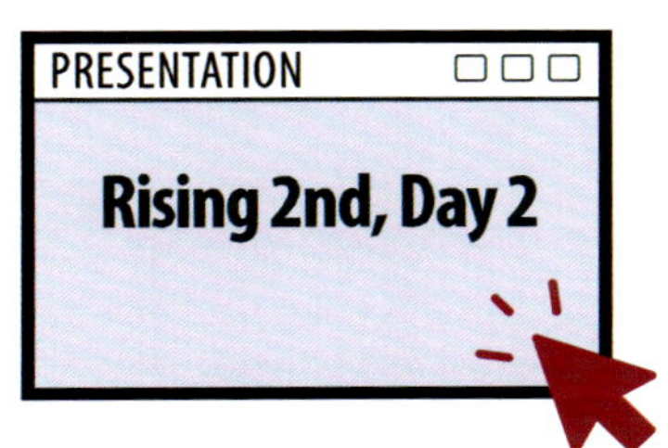

## Read Pattern Words

Now, we're going to read closed syllable words. When I show you a word, follow these steps:

1. Point to the vowels. Say the number of vowels.
2. If the vowel is followed by 1 or more consonants, say "yes." Say "no" if it is not.
3. Say the syllable type and show the gesture.
4. Say the vowel sound and keyword.
5. Read the word.

### Answer Key

| Words on Presentation | |
|---|---|
| 1. (1, yes, closed, /ă/ apple) - bat | 6. (1, yes, closed, /ŭ/ up) - run |
| 2. (1, yes, closed, /ĭ/ itch) - fin | 7. (1, yes, closed, /ĭ/ itch) - hid |
| 3. (1, yes, closed, /ŭ/ up) - cut | 8. (1, yes, closed, /ĕ/ echo) - ten |
| 4. (1, yes, closed, /ĕ/ echo) - bet | 9. (1, yes, closed, /ă/ apple) - had |
| 5. (1, yes, closed, /ŏ/ octopus) - top | 10. (1, yes, closed, /ŏ/ octopus) - cot |

**Routine for Word Sorting:**
- Find the vowels.
- How many vowel letters?
- Is it followed by 1 or more consonants?
- Syllable type and gesture?
- Vowel sound?
- Word?

| | |
|---|---|
| 1. bat | 6. run |
| 2. fin | 7. hid |
| 3. cut | 8. ten |
| 4. bet | 9. had |
| 5. top | 10. cot |

## Phonics Pattern

### SORT WORDS

Let's practice identifying words with each of the short vowel sounds.

Watch what I do.

The first word is <u>men</u>.
- First, I find the vowel and identify the syllable type.
- I see 1 vowel letter *e* followed by 1 consonant.
- This word follows the closed syllable pattern.
- I whisper "closed" while making the closed syllable gesture.
- Then, I whisper the vowel sound /ĕ/.
- I place the word *men* in the /ĕ/ echo column.
- Finally, I slide a finger under the word and whisper "men."

| ă | ĕ | ĭ | ŏ | ŭ |
|---|---|---|---|---|
| | men | | | |



95 Phonics Booster Bundle™: Summer School Edition 2021 • Rising Second • Teacher's Edition

Now it's your turn. Turn to page 5 in your Student Workbook. Let's review the steps.

1. Look at the word to decide which short vowel is in the word.
2. Whisper the syllable type and gesture.
3. Say the vowel sound.
4. Write the word in the correct column.
5. Finally, whisper read all the words in each column.

I'll check back with you in a few minutes and then you can check your answers.

**Answer Key**

| ă  | ĕ | ĭ | ŏ | ŭ |
|---|---|---|---|---|
| an | men | fit | cob | cub |
| fan | pet | in | hot | hut |
| man | | pig | got | |

**Routine for Word Sorting:**

- Find the vowels.
- How many vowel letters?
- Is it followed by 1 or more consonants?
- Syllable type and gesture?
- Vowel sound?
- Where does this word go?
- Read the words.

| | |
|---|---|
| 1. fit | 7. fan |
| 2. an | 8. hot |
| 3. pet | 9. hut |
| 4. cub | 10. man |
| 5. in | 11. pig |
| 6. cob | 12. got |

## Writing

### SOUND-SPELLING MAPPING WITH STUDENT PHONICS CHIPS

Today we will learn how to use colored sound chips to represent sounds in a word.

(Display Sound-Spelling Mat and sound chips.)
- The blue chips represent consonant sounds.
- The red chip represents a short vowel sound.

Repeat after me.
- The blue chips are for consonant sounds. The blue chips are for consonant sounds.
- The red chip is for short vowel sounds. The red chip is for short vowel sounds.

We're going to practice moving sound chips into boxes and then writing the letters to spell the words.

Watch me, my turn.

The first word is <u>van</u>.

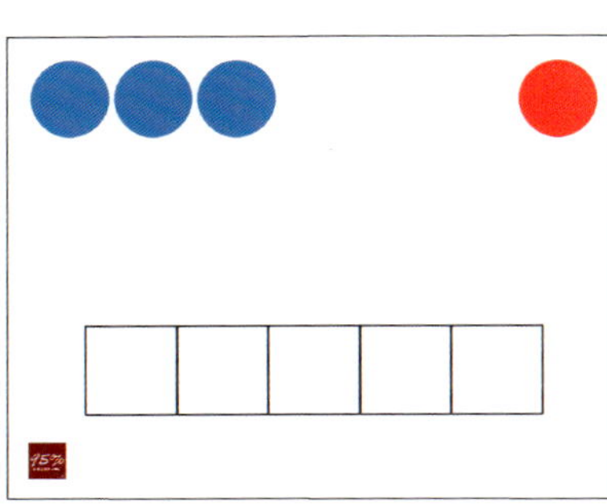

## Chips

- **First, I finger-stretch and say the sounds. I put my hand in a fist, and starting with my thumb, I "stretch" 1 finger for each sound.** (Be sure the students are seeing you stretch the sounds left to right to mimic reading directionality.) **/v/ /ă/ /n/**
- **There are 3 sounds. I need 3 boxes for the 3 sounds. I'll place a dot in the bottom right corner of each box as I say the sounds. /v/ /ă/ /n/**
- **Now, I move chips into the boxes to represent the sounds. Remember, blue chips represent consonant sounds, and the red chip represents short vowel sounds.**
  - **The first sound is /v/. This is a consonant sound so I pull down a blue chip.**
  - **The middle sound is /ă/. This a short vowel sound so I pull down the red chip.**
  - **The last sound is /n/. This is a consonant sound so I pull down another blue chip.**
- **The sounds are /v/ /ă/ /n/.** (Touch under each chip as you say the sounds.)
- **The word is van.** (Slide your finger under the chips.)

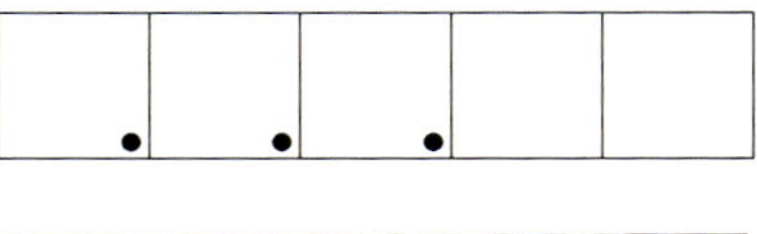

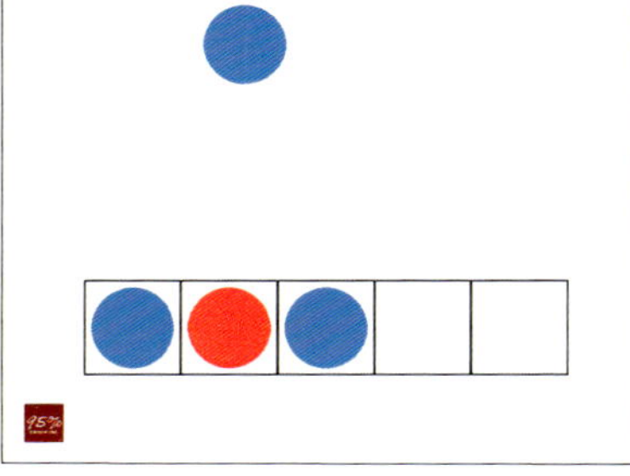

## Letters

- **Now, watch me write the letters that represent each sound.**
  - **The /v/ sound is spelled with the letter _v_, so I write it in the first box.**
  - **The /ă/ sound is spelled with the letter _a_, so I write it in the second box.**
  - **The /n/ sound is spelled with the letter _n_, so I write it in the third box.**
- **The word _van_ is a closed syllable because it has 1 vowel letter followed by 1 consonant.** (Make the closed syllable gesture under the word _van_.)
- **Let's review all the sounds: /v/ /ă/ /n/.** (Touch under each letter as you say the sounds.)
- **The word is van.** (Slide your finger under the word.)

**Let's do the next one together. Watch me move the chips and write the letters.** (Answer with the students.)

**The word is <u>set</u>. Word?** set

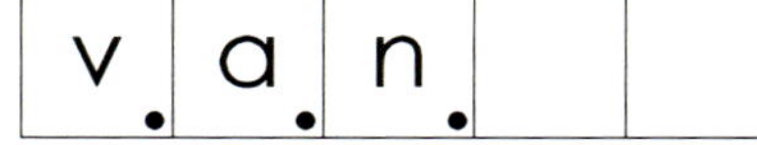

## Chips

- **Finger-stretch set.** /s/ /ĕ/ /t/
- **How many sounds?** 3 **How many boxes should I dot?** 3
- **First sound?** /s/ **Chip?** blue
- **Middle sound?** /ĕ/ **Chip?** red
- **Last sound?** /t/ **Chip?** blue
- **Sounds?** /s/ /ĕ/ /t/
- **Vowel sound?** /ĕ/ **Is it a short vowel sound?** yes

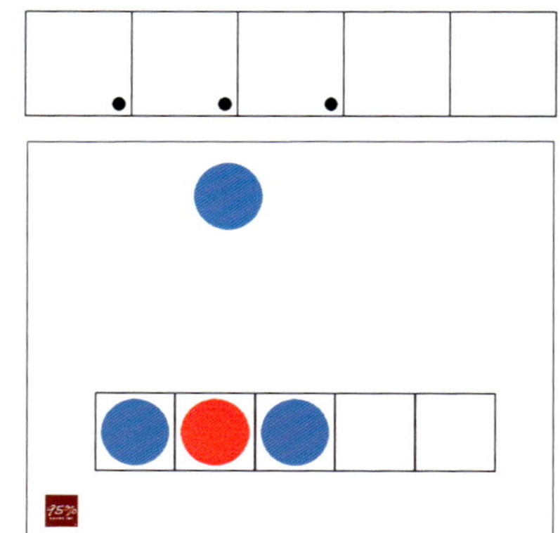

**Letters**
- **Which letter spells the /s/ sound?** s
- **Which letter spells the /ĕ/ sound?** e
- **Which letter spells the /t/ sound?** t
- **Does this follow the closed syllable pattern?** yes **How do you know?** 1 vowel followed by 1 or more consonants
- **Sounds?** /s/ /ĕ/ /t/
- **Word?** set

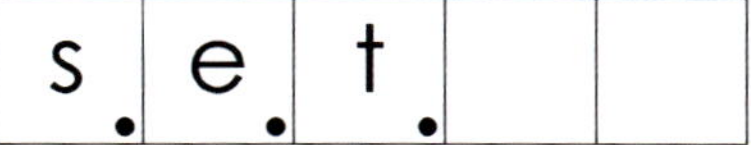

Now it's your turn. Get your chips and mat ready. Place the blue consonant chips on the left side and the red vowel chip on the right side. Lay out the following chips on your mat:
- **3 blue chips**
- **1 red chip**

**Does your mat look like this?**

**What type of sound do the blue chips represent?** consonant
**What type of sound does the red chip represent?** short vowel

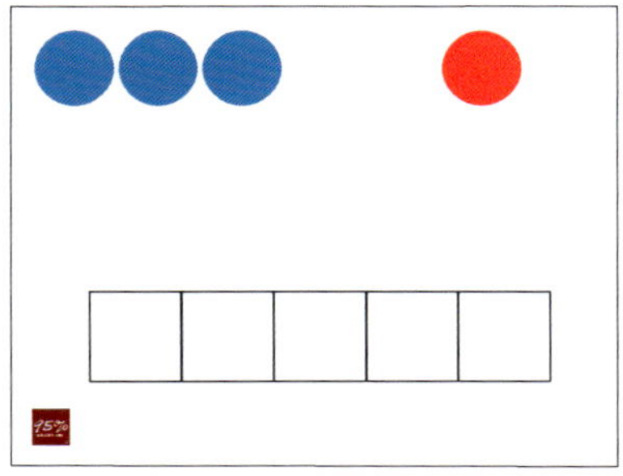

 **Turn to page 5 in your Student Workbook. Here are the steps:**

1. **I'm going to say a word and you'll repeat it.**
2. **Finger-stretch the sounds and place dots in your workbook.**
3. **Then, move chips on your mat.**
4. **Write the letters in your workbook.**
5. **Finally, whisper read the word.**

| Words to Dictate | Placement of Phonics Chips on Mat | Correct Answers in Student Workbook |
|---|---|---|
| set | 🔵🔴🔵 | s e t |
| 1. him | 🔵🔴🔵 | h i m |
| 2. got | 🔵🔴🔵 | g o t |
| 3. sat | 🔵🔴🔵 | s a t |
| 4. run | 🔵🔴🔵 | r u n |
| 5. did | 🔵🔴🔵 | d i d |

🔑 **Routine for Chip Movement:**

- **Finger-stretch sounds.**
  - **How many sounds?**
  - **How many boxes?**
  - **Dot boxes in workbook.**
- **Sound? Chip?** (repeat for each sound)
- **Which letter spells the /_/ sound?** (repeat for each sound)
- **Word?**

**Day 2**

## Passage Reading

### READ PASSAGE

**Passage – Literary: *Gus and Peg***

Now we'll read the passage we underlined and circled yesterday. This passage is about 2 cats named Gus and Peg.

First, we'll read some of the underlined and circled words together. When you see an underlined or circled closed syllable word, make the closed syllable gesture and read the word. What are the underlined words in the title? Gus, and, Peg Read with me just the underlined and circled words above the black line.

Now it's your turn. Turn to page 4 in your Student Workbook. Here are the steps:

1. First, whisper read all the underlined words in the rest of the passage.
2. Then, go back to the beginning and whisper read the passage.

## Comprehension

### WRITTEN RESPONSE

Turn to page 5 in your Student Workbook. Use the graphic organizer to make short notes about 1 detail that happened in the beginning, middle, and end of this passage. I will give you 5 minutes and then I will ask a few of you to share.

**Answer Key** (answers vary)

| Beginning | Middle | End |
|---|---|---|
| Gus is the little cat who likes to hop and run. Peg is the big cat who likes to run and dig. | Gus and Peg like catnip. They hop on the bed to get the catnip. | Gus and Peg play a lot and this keeps them fit. |

## DAY 3

### Phonological Awareness Warm-Up

Today we are going to practice <u>phoneme segmentation</u>. Let's review the instructions:

- I'll say a word and you repeat it.
- Then, tell me the sounds in the word. Ready?

| | | | |
|---|---|---|---|
| Say cloud: (**cloud**) Sounds? | /k/ /l/ /ou/ /d/ | Say stay: (**stay**) Sounds? | /s/ /t/ /ā/ |
| Say spot: (**spot**) Sounds? | /s/ /p/ /ŏ/ /t/ | Say cheese: (**cheese**) Sounds? | /ch/ /ē/ /z/ |
| Say cry: (**cry**) Sounds? | /k/ /r/ /ī/ | Say run: (**run**) Sounds? | /r/ /ŭ/ /n/ |
| Say snap: (**snap**) Sounds? | /s/ /n/ /ă/ /p/ | Say slip: (**slip**) Sounds? | /s/ /l/ /ĭ/ /p/ |
| Say rain: (**rain**) Sounds? | /r/ /ā/ /n/ | Say cape: (**cape**) Sounds? | /k/ /ā/ /p/ |
| Say stripe: (**stripe**) Sounds? | /s/ /t/ /r/ /ī/ /p/ | Say bright: (**bright**) Sounds? | /b/ /r/ /ī/ /t/ |
| Say face: (**face**) Sounds? | /f/ /ā/ /s/ | Say sand: (**sand**) Sounds? | /s/ /ă/ /n/ /d/ |
| Say class: (**class**) Sounds? | /k/ /l/ /ă/ /s/ | Say chat: (**chat**) Sounds? | /ch/ /ă/ /t/ |

## Phonics Pattern

### WORD READING ACCURACY

**Look at the words. Let's read them together. Since each word follows the closed syllable pattern, hold up the closed gesture as you read each word.**

| | | | |
|---|---|---|---|
| bad | red | men | had |
| did | rub | job | sit |
| but | beg | can | run |
| hot | pop | mug | got |
| sat | win | his | net |

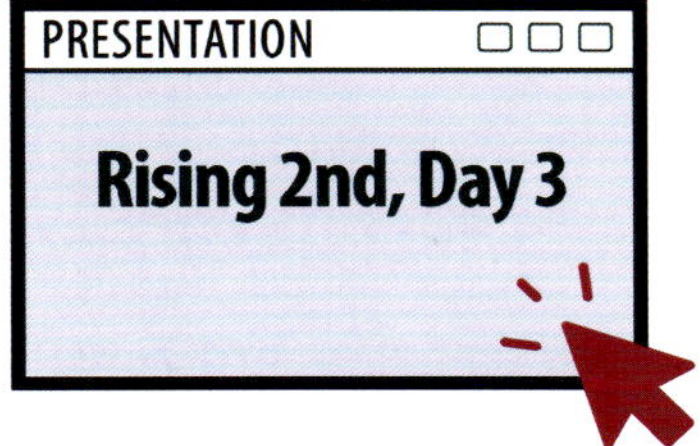


## Writing

### FIND PATTERN WORDS IN SENTENCES

**Now we're going to look for pattern words in sentences. First, I'll read a sentence. Next, I'll go back to circle the closed syllable words. Then, I'll write the closed syllable words on the lines.**

**Before we begin, let's review the pattern for a closed syllable word.**

**A closed syllable has (say it with me): 1 vowel letter followed by 1 or more consonants, and the vowel sound is short**

**Watch the steps I use.** (Display sentence.)

The man sat on the log.

**I circle the following closed syllable words: man, sat, on, and log. Then, I write those 4 words on the lines below the sentence.**

The (man)(sat)(on) the (log).
man  sat  on  log

**Day 3**

**Now it's your turn. Turn to page 6 in your Student Workbook. Let's review the steps.**

1. **Read the sentence.**
2. **Circle the closed syllable words.**
3. **Write the closed pattern words on the lines below the sentence.**

**I'll give you a few minutes and then we'll check them together.**

### Answer Key

1. The (vet)(has) a (red)(pen.)   vet  has  red  pen
2. The (hut)(is)(hot) from the (sun.)   hut  is  hot  sun

*Note:* The word *from* does not have the short o sound and is not considered a pattern word.

---

## Writing

### SOUND-SPELLING MAPPING WITH STUDENT PHONICS CHIPS

We've done sound-spelling mapping before so I'll briefly review the steps before you begin. Remember, the blue chips represent consonants and the red chip represents a short vowel.

Let's do one together. Watch me move the chips and write the letters.

The word is <u>beg</u>. Word? **beg**

**Chips**

- **Finger-stretch beg. /b/ /ĕ/ /g/**
- **How many sounds? 3 How many boxes should I dot? 3**
- **First sound? /b/ Chip? blue**
- **Middle sound? /ĕ/ Chip? red**
- **Last sound? /g/ Chip? blue**
- **Vowel sound? /ĕ/ Is it a short vowel sound? yes**
- **Sounds? /b/ /ĕ/ /g/ Word? beg**

**Letters**

- **Which letter spells the /b/ sound? b**
- **Which letter spells the /ĕ/ sound? e**
- **Which letter spells the /g/ sound? g**
- **Syllable type and gesture? closed**
- **Sounds? /b/ /ĕ/ /g/**
- **Word? beg**

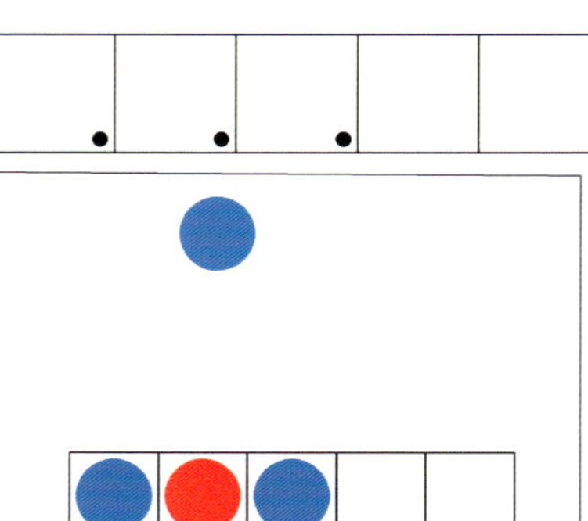

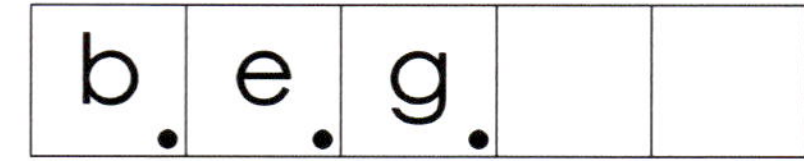

Now it's your turn. Get your chips and mat ready. Remember to place the blue consonant chips on the left side, and the red short vowel chip on the right side. Lay the following chips on your mat:

- 3 blue chips
- 1 red chip

Does your mat look like this?

What type of sound do the blue chips represent? **consonant**
What type of sound does the red chip represent? **short vowel**

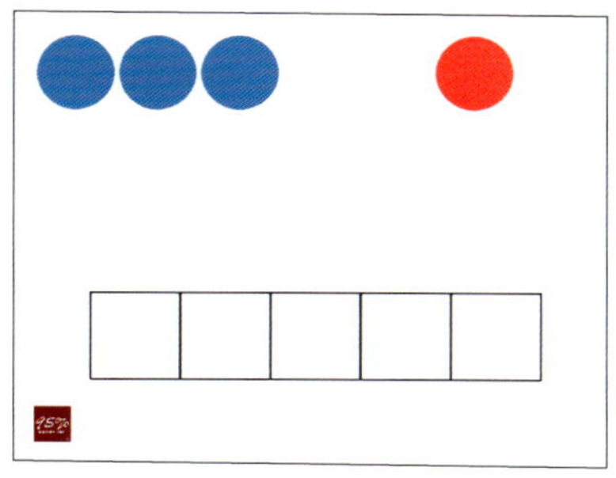

 **Turn to page 6 in your Student Workbook. Here are the steps:**

1. I'm going to say a word and you'll repeat it.
2. Finger-stretch the sounds and place dots in your workbook.
3. Then, move chips on your mat.
4. Write the letters in your workbook.
5. Finally, whisper read the word.

## Answer Key

| Words to Dictate | Placement of Phonics Chips on Mat | Correct Answers in Student Workbook |
|---|---|---|
| beg | 🔵🔴🔵 | b. e. g. |
| 1. dad | 🔵🔴🔵 | d. a. d. |
| 2. leg | 🔵🔴🔵 | l. e. g. |
| 3. sat | 🔵🔴🔵 | s. a. t. |
| 4. lot | 🔵🔴🔵 | l. o. t. |
| 5. rug | 🔵🔴🔵 | r. u. g. |

**🔑 Routine for Chip Movement:**

- **Finger-stretch sounds.**
  – How many sounds?
  – How many boxes?
  – Dot boxes in workbook.
- **Sound? Chip?** (repeat for each sound)
- **Which letter spells the /_/ sound?** (repeat for each sound)
- **Word?**

 95 Phonics Booster Bundle™: Summer School Edition 2021 • Rising Second • Teacher's Edition **17**

Day
3

## Phonics Pattern

### READING MULTISYLLABLE WORDS

**Let me show you the routine for reading multisyllable words.**

(Display catnip.)
**Here is the first word.** (Do not read the word.)

**Step 1: Find the vowels.**
- **I use both hands to find the vowels in each syllable.**
- **I point to the letter *a* with my left pointer finger, and the letter *i* with my right pointer finger.**
- **There are 2 vowel sounds.**

catnip

**Step 2: Underline the vowels.**
- **Next, I underline the vowels.**
- **This word has 2 syllables because it has 2 vowel sounds.**

catnip

**Step 3: Draw a line between the syllables.**
- **I look for the number of consonants between the vowels.**
- **There are 2—t and n. Most often when there are 2 consonants between the 2 vowels, we will divide the word between them.**
- **I draw a syllable division line between the letters *t* and *n*.**

cat|nip

**Step 4: Read each syllable.**

| Read the first syllable. 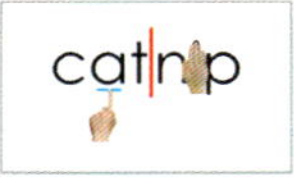 | Read the second syllable.  |
|---|---|
| **I cover the second syllable and look at the first one.**<br>• **The syllable type is closed.**<br>• **The vowel sound is /ă/.**<br>• **The syllable is cat.** | **I cover the first syllable and look at the second one.**<br>• **The syllable type is closed.**<br>• **The vowel sound is /ĭ/.**<br>• **The syllable is nip.** |

**Step 5: Read the word.**
- **The word is catnip.**

**Now we'll do 2 more words together. When I show you a word, answer my questions and I will show you what to do.** (Students should be pointing towards the displayed words and gesturing throughout the routine.)

(Display sunset.)
**Here is the next word.** (Do not read the word.)

**Step 1: Find the vowels.**
- **Use both hands to find the vowels in each syllable.**
- **Point to the letter *u* with the left pointer finger, and the letter *e* with the right pointer finger.**
- **How many vowel sounds? 2**

sunset

**Step 2: Underline the vowels.**
- Next, I underline the vowels.
- This word has 2 vowel sounds. How many syllables? **2**

sunset

**Step 3: Draw a line between the syllables.**
- How many consonants are between the 2 vowel sounds? **2**
- Yes, there are 2—n and s. When there are 2 consonants between the 2 vowels, divide the word between them.
- Where do I draw the line? **between the letters *n* and *s***
- I draw a syllable division line between the letters *n* and *s*.

sun|set

**Step 4: Read each syllable.**

| Read the first syllable.  | Read the second syllable.  |
|---|---|
| I cover the second syllable and look at the first one. <br>• Syllable type? **closed** <br>• Vowel sound? **/ŭ/** <br>• Syllable? **sun** | I cover the first syllable and look at the second one. <br>• Syllable type? **closed** <br>• Vowel sound? **/ĕ/** <br>• Syllable? **set** |

**Step 5: Read the word.**
- Word? **sunset**

(Display kitten.)
**Here is the last word we will do together.** (Do not read the word.)

**Step 1: Find the vowels.**
- Use both hands to find the vowels in each syllable.
- Point to the letter *i* with the left pointer finger, and the letter *e* with the right pointer finger.
- How many vowel sounds are there? **2**

kitten

**Step 2: Underline the vowels.**
- Next, I underline the vowels.
- There are 2 vowel sounds. How many syllables are there? **2**

kitten

**Step 3: Draw a line between the syllables.**
- How many consonants are between the 2 vowel sounds? **2**
- There are 2—t and t. When there are 2 consonants between the 2 vowels, divide the word between them.
- Where do I draw the line? **between the letters *t* and *t***
- I draw a syllable division line between the letters *t* and *t*.

kit|ten

---

**Day 3**

## Step 4: Read each syllable.

| Read the first syllable.<br><br>I cover the second syllable and look at the first one.<br>• Syllable type? **closed**<br>• Vowel sound? **/ĭ/**<br>• Syllable? **kit** |  | Read the second syllable.<br><br>I cover the first syllable and look at the second one.<br>• Syllable type? **closed**<br>• Vowel sound? **/ĕ/**<br>• Syllable? **ten** |  |

## Step 5: Read the word.
• **Word? kitten**

## Passage Reading

### UNDERLINE/CIRCLE PATTERN WORDS

### Passage – Informational: *The Canyon*

Now it's time to practice with a new passage. This passage is about visiting a big canyon. Do you know what a canyon is? A canyon is a large dip in the earth caused by weather or rivers.

Today we are going to look for closed syllable words with a short vowel sound. We will also circle 2-syllable words that have 2 closed syllables. Let's begin with the title. Which is the first word to underline or circle? **canyon** Do we underline or circle it? **circle** Why? **It is a 2-syllable word with the closed syllable pattern.**

Help me find more words to underline and circle. If you see a word with the closed syllable pattern, hold up the closed syllable gesture; I'll underline it if it has 1 syllable, or circle it if there are 2 syllables in the word. (Continue underlining and circling the closed syllable words to the black line.)

 Now it's your turn. Turn to page 7 in your Student Workbook. Here are the steps:

1. Begin below the black line where none of the words are underlined or circled.
2. Look at each word and point to the vowel or vowels.
3. If the word has the closed syllable pattern, underline it if it has 1 syllable or circle it if it has 2 syllables.
4. Finally, whisper read the words you underlined and circled.

(Refer to the note under the passage on page 3 for exceptions.)

I'll give you a few minutes and we'll check them together.

*Note:* The second syllable of the word *canyon* is an unstressed syllable and the vowel *o* is pronounced with a schwa sound  (/ə/). The schwa sound is pronounced with a reduced short u sound.

# DAY 4

## Phonological Awareness Warm-Up

Today we are going to practice <u>phoneme segmentation</u>. Let's review the instructions:
- I'll say a word and you repeat it.
- Then, tell me the sounds in the word. Ready?

| | | | |
|---|---|---|---|
| Say smile: (smile) Sounds? | /s/ /m/ /ī/ /l/ | Say bike: (bike) Sounds? | /b/ /ī/ /k/ |
| Say flash: (flash) Sounds? | /f/ /l/ /ă/ /sh/ | Say spin: (spin) Sounds? | /s/ /p/ /ĭ/ /n/ |
| Say right: (right) Sounds? | /r/ /ī/ /t/ | Say glass: (glass) Sounds? | /g/ /l/ /ă/ /s/ |
| Say back: (back) Sounds? | /b/ /ă/ /k/ | Say head: (head) Sounds? | /h/ /ĕ/ /d/ |
| Say nose: (nose) Sounds? | /n/ /ō/ /z/ | Say free: (free) Sounds? | /f/ /r/ /ē/ |
| Say hug: (hug) Sounds? | /h/ /ŭ/ /g/ | Say cake: (cake) Sounds? | /k/ /ā/ /k/ |
| Say chip: (chip) Sounds? | /ch/ /ĭ/ /p/ | Say rise: (rise) Sounds? | /r/ /ī/ /z/ |
| Say green: (green) Sounds? | /g/ /r/ /ē/ /n/ | Say bug: (bug) Sounds? | /b/ /ŭ/ /g/ |

## Fluency

### HIGH-FREQUENCY WORDS

Display the high-frequency word grid. Prompt students by saying **"Word?"**

| | | | |
|---|---|---|---|
| were | them | could | when |
| as | then | had | some |
| her | him | of | his |
| said | they | four | well |

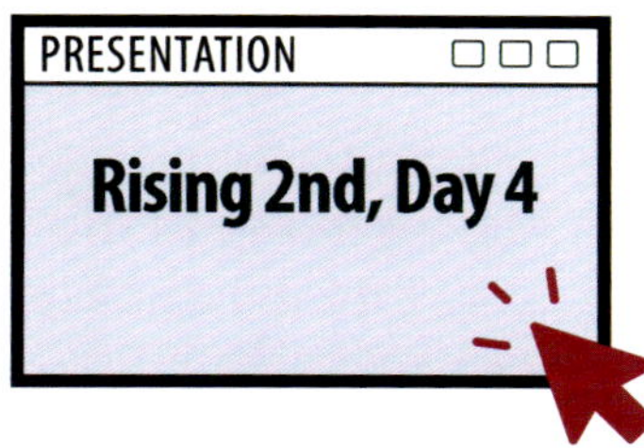


**Now it's your turn. Turn to page 7 in your Student Workbook. When I say "begin," point to the first word and whisper it. Continue reading across the page. If you finish before I say "stop," start at the top and read the words again.** (Time students for 1 minute. Say "stop" and ask students to circle the last word that was read.)

| | | | |
|---|---|---|---|
| could | had | his | then |
| said | as | were | well |
| some | four | they | her |
| them | of | him | when |

 95 Phonics Booster Bundle™: Summer School Edition 2021 • Rising Second • Teacher's Edition 

## Writing

### INFLECTED ENDINGS

Now we will review the past tense ending *-ed*. Past tense is when a verb, which is an action word, changes to indicate that something happened in the past. The verb changes from present tense to past tense when the ending *-ed* is added.

There are 3 rules about how a spelling changes when the past tense ending *-ed* is added at the end of a verb.

(Display the Spelling Rules table.) **Look at this table that summarizes the 3 spelling rules.**

| Rule | Verb | New Word | Spelling Rules |
|------|------|----------|----------------|
| 1 | fish | fished | Verb spelled with a vowel team, ends in y, or has 2 consonants at the end, add -ed |
| 2 | bake | baked | Verb spelled with the silent-e pattern, drop the last e before adding -ed |
| 3 | tap | tapped | Verb spelled with 1 vowel followed by 1 consonant, the final consonant is doubled before adding -ed |

**We will only practice rule 3 today. Watch what I do.**

**The word is fit.** (Display fit.)

- **I find the vowel and touch under it.**
- **The word *fit* has 1 vowel followed by 1 consonant. It is similar to the word *tap* in the table, which also has 1 vowel followed by 1 consonant. I double the final consonant when adding the -ed ending.**
- **The new word is fitted, which I write in the column labeled "New Word + ed."**

 **Turn to page 8 in your Student Workbook. Here are the steps:**

1. **Find the vowel in the word.**
2. **If the word has 1 vowel followed by 1 consonant, double the consonant at the end and add -ed.**
3. **Write the new word in the "New Word + ed" column.**
4. **Whisper read the new word to yourself.**

## Answer Key

| Verb | New Word + ed |
|------|---------------|
| fit | fitted |
| 1. lug | lugged |
| 2. jog | jogged |
| 3. jet | jetted |
| 4. bat | batted |

## Writing

### WORD CHAINS

It's word chain time! In this routine, we will create a "chain" of words by adding, deleting, or changing 1 sound at a time to spell a new word.

Let's do this first one together.

**The first word is <u>sat</u>.**

**Let's change <u>sat</u> to <u>set</u>.**
- **Which sound changes?** /ă/ changes to /ĕ/
- **Which letter changes?** change the letter *a* to *e*

I write the word *set* under *sat*.

**Next, I change <u>set</u> to <u>sit</u>.**
- **Which sound changes?** /ĕ/ changes to /ĭ/
- **Which letter changes?** change the letter *e* to *i*

I write the word *sit* under *set*.

**Finally, I change <u>sit</u> to <u>kit</u>.**
- **Which sound changes?** /s/ changes to /k/
- **Which letter changes?** change the letter *s* to *k*

I write the word *kit* under *sit*.

 **Now it's your turn. Turn to page 8 in your Student Workbook. You'll find a spot to write 3 word chains. I'll tell you 1 word at a time and you'll write each new word below the old one. Find the page and look up when you're ready.**

| sat |
|-----|
| set |
| sit |
| kit |

***Note:*** If you are writing the words on the board, make sure you build the words going down, not across.

 **Routine for Word Chains:**

- **Change word *x* to word *y*.**
  - **Which sound changes?**
  - **Which letter(s) changes?**
- **Write word *y* under word *x*.**

Day 4

## Answer Key

| | | |
|---|---|---|
| pig | bag | lit |
| peg | bug | hit |
| pen | bog | hot |
| pan | big | hop |

## Passage Reading

### READ PASSAGE

### Passage – Informational: *The Canyon*

Now it's time to read a passage, *The Canyon*. Do you remember what a canyon is? A canyon is a gap or break in the earth caused by weather or a river.

 Turn to page 7 in your Student Workbook. First, we will read the passage aloud together. While we're reading, think about the main topic of the passage. The main topic tells what the passage is mostly about. (Guide students in chorally reading the passage, starting with the title.)

## Comprehension

### WRITTEN RESPONSE

Turn to page 8 in your Student Workbook. There is a graphic organizer we will complete together.

- **What is the title of the passage we read today?** The Canyon
  **Please write the title in the top box of your graphic organizer.**
- **What is the main topic of this passage?** (answers vary)
  - **I find that the first sentence of the passage tells the main topic: "I get to go to a big canyon with my sis, Val."**
  - **I write this idea in my own words: A trip to visit the big canyon with Val.**
  - **Please write this in your graphic organizer in the space under Main Topic.**
- **What are some things that we learned about a canyon from the passage?** (answers vary: canyons have rims, canyons have pretty sunsets, the pits can be red and yellow, canyons are dim when the sun sets, etc.)
  - **Add 3 of those details to the graphic organizer in your workbook. Use complete sentences with a capital at the beginning and correct punctuation at the end.**

**Note:** You might choose to write the details the students share on a whiteboard or chart paper. This will provide support for the students when they are completing the Key Details portion of the graphic organizer.

 95 Phonics Booster Bundle™: Summer School Edition 2021 • Rising Second • Teacher's Edition

| Title: The Canyon | |
| --- | --- |
| **Main Topic** | |
| A trip to visit the big canyon with Val. | |
| **Key Details** | |
| 1. | |
| 2. | |
| 3. | |

## DAY 5

### Phonological Awareness Warm-Up

Today we are going to practice <u>phoneme segmentation</u>. Let's review the instructions:

- **I'll say a word and you repeat it.**
- **Then, tell me the sounds in the word. Ready?**

| | | | |
| --- | --- | --- | --- |
| Say teeth: (**teeth**) Sounds? | /t/ /ē/ /th/ | Say shade: (**shade**) Sounds? | /sh/ /ā/ /d/ |
| Say find: (**find**) Sounds? | /f/ /ī/ /n/ /d/ | Say sleep: (**sleep**) Sounds? | /s/ /l/ /ē/ /p/ |
| Say flag: (**flag**) Sounds? | /f/ /l/ /ă/ /g/ | Say desk: (**desk**) Sounds? | /d/ /ĕ/ /s/ /k/ |
| Say hole: (**hole**) Sounds? | /h/ /ō/ /l/ | Say cute: (**cute**) Sounds? | /k/ /yū/ /t/ |
| Say home: (**home**) Sounds? | /h/ /ō/ /m/ | Say time: (**time**) Sounds? | /t/ /ī/ /m/ |
| Say coat: (**coat**) Sounds? | /k/ /ō/ /t/ | Say duck: (**duck**) Sounds? | /d/ /ŭ/ /k/ |
| Say paint: (**paint**) Sounds? | /p/ /ā/ /n/ /t/ | Say road: (**road**) Sounds? | /r/ /ō/ /d/ |
| Say bed: (**bed**) Sounds? | /b/ /ĕ/ /d/ | Say tent: (**tent**) Sounds? | /t/ /ĕ/ /n/ /t/ |

### Writing

#### SOUND-SPELLING MAPPING

Now we're going to spell words that have the closed syllable pattern. We've spelled words using the sound-spelling boxes and chips before. Today we will do sound-spelling mapping without using chips. Remember, each box holds 1 sound. Let's do one together.

The word is <u>wet</u>. Word? **wet**
- **Finger-stretch and say the sounds.** /w/ /ĕ/ /t/
- **How many sounds? 3 How many boxes? 3**
- **We need 3 boxes. I tap and mark a dot in the bottom right corner for each sound.** /w/ /ĕ/ /t/

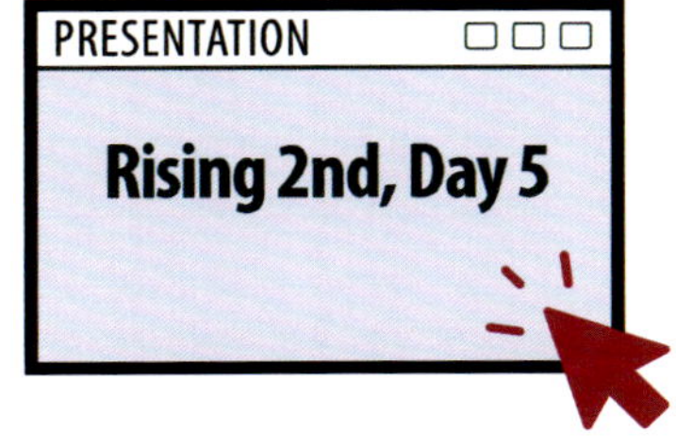


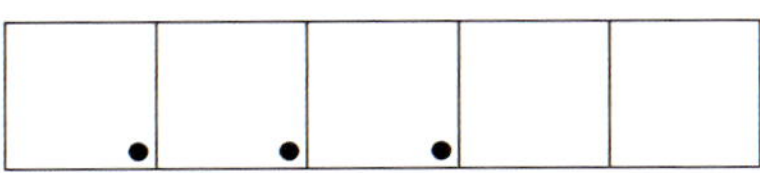

**Day 5**

- Now, I write the letters.
  - Which letter spells the /w/ sound? **w** Where do I write it? **in the first box**
  - Which letter spells the /ĕ/ sound? **e** Where do I write it? **in the second box**
  - Which letter spells the /t/ sound? **t** Where do I write it? **in the third box**
- Syllable type and gesture? **closed**
- Sounds? **/w/ /ĕ/ /t/**
- Word? **wet**

 Now it's your turn. Turn to page 9 in your Student Workbook. Here are the steps:

1. Finger-stretch while saying the sounds.
2. Count the sounds.
3. Place a dot in the bottom right corner of the boxes you'll need.
4. Write the letters. Remember that each sound gets its own box.
5. Whisper the syllable type and read the word to yourself.

**Answer Key**

| Words to Dictate | Correct Answers in Student Workbook |
|---|---|
| wet | w e t |
| 1. at | a t |
| 2. kid | k i d |
| 3. met | m e t |
| 4. bus | b u s |
| 5. mom | m o m |

**Note:** The Floss Rule is when a short vowel is followed by f, l, s or z, the consonant is doubled (e.g., stuff, pill, dress, fuzz). The word *bus* (#4) appears to break the Floss Rule. The word *bus* is an abbreviation for omnibus, just as gas is an abbreviation for gasoline. Therefore, these words are not exceptions to this rule.

Day
5

## Writing

### SENTENCE DICTATION

On page 9 of your Student Workbook, there are some lines to write sentences. I'll tell you a sentence. Repeat it. Then write it and we'll check it together.

First sentence: <u>Bob is a big dog.</u> Repeat it with me. Now write it.

Now let's check it. Look at the sentence. Place a dot under each letter and punctuation mark if you got it right. Correct it, if needed.

Second sentence: <u>My cat is on the rug.</u> Repeat it with me. Now write it. (Repeat the correction procedure above.)

Third sentence: <u>Ed and Bev have a pig.</u> Repeat it with me. Now write it. (Repeat the correction procedure above.)

## Fluency

### PHRASES

Next we're going to read phrases. Let's practice 4 phrases together.

| by the dog | mom will go | look at the dot | in my hot rod |

Now it's your turn. Turn to page 10 in your Student Workbook. When I say "begin," point to the first phrase and whisper it. Continue reading across the page. If you finish before I say "stop," start at the top and read the phrases again. (Time students for 1 minute. Say "stop" and ask students to circle the last phrase that was read.)

| under the log | a good job | go for a jog | some are hot |
|---|---|---|---|
| in the hut | is my pet | to the tub | were they wet |
| in the pot | on the log | said the man | had a bat |
| at the vet | see the sun | for the pigs | her new kit |

**Day 5**

## Passage Reading

### READ PASSAGES

Today you are going to practice reading both of the passages. One was about a kid and 2 cats. The second was about a visit to a big canyon.

## Comprehension

### WRITTEN RESPONSE

Turn to page 10 in your Student Workbook. Read both passages, and then write the answers to the question for each passage in your workbook.

**Passage – Literary: *Gus and Peg* on page 4**
1. **Who is the little cat? Who is the big cat?  (RL.1.1)**  (Gus is the little cat. Peg is the big cat.)

**Passage – Informational: *The Canyon* on page 7**
1. **What will the canyon look like at sunset? (RI.1.1)**  (The canyon will look pretty. It will be red and yellow in the pit.)

---

 **Teacher Tip**

Resist the temptation to skip the phonological awareness warm-up. Daily exposure to thinking about sounds in words is critical for later word learning. As this program progresses, students will begin to practice manipulating phonemes (addition and substitution). Mastery of the more advanced phonemic awareness is the goal. Remember that this is an auditory activity without print.

---

 **Teacher Tip**

You just completed the first 5 days in the program. By reviewing each short vowel sound and the closed syllable pattern, students are now prepared to progress through the next 10 lessons in Days 6–15. These lessons will continue to reinforce short vowels in combination with consonant blends and digraphs.

### Multisyllable Words

During the Day 3 lesson, there was an introduction to reading simple closed-closed multisyllable words; the teacher demonstrated with 3 words, 2 of which were compound words (catnip and sunset) and 1 which was a common noun (kitten). The only words included followed the "simple" division rule where there are only 2 consonants between the vowels so the word is divided between the 2 consonants; each syllable is a closed syllable.

This introduction on how to read multisyllable words was included in the Day 3 lesson because students will find multisyllable words in many of the authentic texts as they rise up to second grade; additionally, when universal screening assessments are given, students will be required to read multisyllable words in the passages. This program will include instruction on multisyllable words with the closed, silent-e, and open syllable types as well as exposure to vowel team and vowel-r syllables.

### Inflected Ending *-ed*

The other skill included in Day 4 was a review of the inflected ending *-ed*. This is a hard concept and students aren't expected to master it with this lesson. They will see it again and practice it more in future lessons.

### Looking Ahead at Days 6–10

Day 6 starts the next section of the program, which covers initial 3-letter blends. There are 5 days of lessons on blends.

While consonant blends appear in words with short, long, vowel team, or vowel-r syllables, all the words included in the blend lessons (Days 6–10) contain only short vowels and are closed syllables. Therefore, the student has many opportunities to master the concept of what a closed syllable is and how it provides guidance to use the short vowel sound when sounding out an unknown word.

The important insight for students in the blend lessons is that each consonant letter in the blend represents a separate sound. The term *blend* can be confusing to students; it implies that the sound is a blended sound when in fact each letter maintains its own sound. Because there is a 1:1 correspondence between letters and sounds, this program teaches consonant blends before consonant digraphs. Students who understand the closed syllable concept should do well on these lessons.

# Mud Splat!

1 Scrapping with mud is a fun craft, but it can be a splat!

2 My mom asked me to scram and go get the tub with the straps.

3 I grabbed the tub straps and sprinted fast.

4 As I sprinted down the steps, I landed with a splat. The tub

5 splashed down. I saw my hand was split. I held a scrap of rag on

6 my hand and set it with a splint. I grabbed a new tub and got a

7 good grip on the straps.

8 I had to scrub the splat of mud. I grabbed a new rag

9 scrap and scrubbed at the spots. I was masked in mud splats! I

10 scrubbed and scrubbed. I stripped away my pants to scrub the

11 last strands of mud on them. Scrapping in mud was a big splat!

| Initial 3-Letter Blends | | Word Count* |
|---|---|---|
| scram | split | 136 |
| scrap | sprint | **Pattern Words** |
| scrub | strand | 26 (19%) |
| splash | strap | * including title |
| splat | strip | |
| splint | | |

# Scrub the Mud Out

1    If you play in mud, you can get splats and spots on you.
2  To get the splats out of pants is a task. Split some rags to make
3  scraps. Rag scraps will help to scrub out the splats.
4    Here is a scripted plan to strip the mud splats that are on
5  pants. One, get a tub of suds. Do not scrimp on the suds. Two,
6  drop the pants with mud splats in the tub. Three, let the pants
7  sit in the suds. Now, a fast scrub with the rag scrap will help
8  strip the splats. Last, grab the pants and strap them up. Are the
9  splats there? If yes, get a tub with suds and scrub the splats and
10  do the steps all over.

| Initial 3-Letter Blends | | Word Count* |
| --- | --- | --- |
| scrap | strip | 128 |
| scrimp | | **Pattern Words** |
| script | | 21 (16%) |
| scrub | | * including title |
| splat | | |
| split | | |

Day
6

# Days 6–10: Initial 3-Letter Blends

## Learning Objective

In Days 6–10, students demonstrate understanding of the initial 3-letter blend pattern in closed syllables by correctly identifying, reading, and writing pattern words in isolation and in passages.

## DAY 6

### Phonological Awareness Warm-Up

**Today we are going to practice <u>phoneme segmentation</u>. Let's review the instructions:**
- **I'll say a word and you repeat it.**
- **Then, tell me the sounds in the word. Ready?**

| | | | |
|---|---|---|---|
| Say shack: (**shack**) Sounds? | /sh/ /ă/ /k/ | Say play: (**play**) Sounds? | /p/ /l/ /ā/ |
| Say flock: (**flock**) Sounds? | /f/ /l/ /ŏ/ /k/ | Say flight: (**flight**) Sounds? | /f/ /l/ /ī/ /t/ |
| Say skit: (**skit**) Sounds? | /s/ /k/ /ĭ/ /t/ | Say black: (**black**) Sounds? | /b/ /l/ /ă/ /k/ |
| Say chat: (**chat**) Sounds? | /ch/ /ă/ /t/ | Say past: (**past**) Sounds? | /p/ /ă/ /s/ /t/ |
| Say ship: (**ship**) Sounds? | /sh/ /ĭ/ /p/ | Say slim: (**slim**) Sounds? | /s/ /l/ /ĭ/ /m/ |
| Say champ: (**champ**) Sounds? | /ch/ /ă/ /m/ /p/ | Say crush: (**crush**) Sounds? | /k/ /r/ /ŭ/ /sh/ |
| Say shell: (**shell**) Sounds? | /sh/ /ĕ/ /l/ | Say house: (**house**) Sounds? | /h/ /ou/ /s/ |
| Say mash: (**mash**) Sounds? | /m/ /ă/ /sh/ | Say shy: (**shy**) Sounds? | /sh/ /ī/ |

## Phonics Pattern

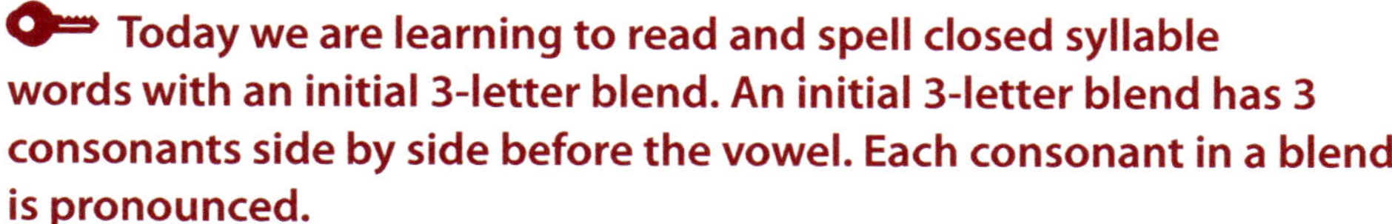

**Today we are learning to read and spell closed syllable words with an initial 3-letter blend. An initial 3-letter blend has 3 consonants side by side before the vowel. Each consonant in a blend is pronounced.**

**Repeat it with me: An initial 3-letter blend has 3 consonants side by side before the vowel. Each consonant in a blend is pronounced.**

**The 3-letter blends in this lesson are in the initial position. If a blend is in the initial position, is it at the beginning or end of a word? the beginning of a word**

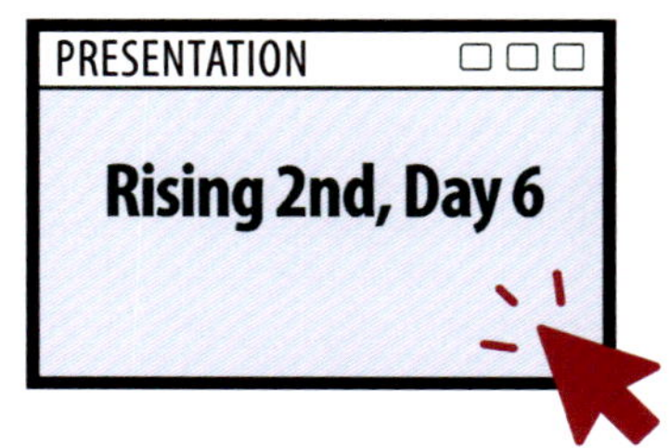

Let's review the closed syllable pattern because the 3-letter blend words that we'll see are all closed syllables. Closed syllable words have 1 vowel letter followed by 1 or more consonants, and the vowel sound is short.

**Repeat it with me:** **Closed syllable words have 1 vowel letter followed by 1 or more consonants, and the vowel sound is short.**

The gesture for the closed syllable is a closed fist.

Practice the gesture with me. 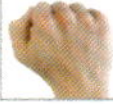 **closed**

## SORT WORDS

(Display sprint.)

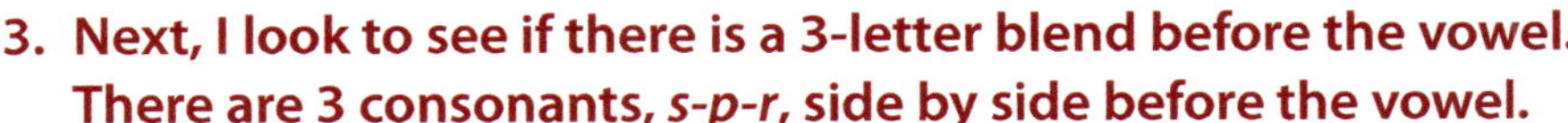 **I'm going to look for the initial 3-letter blend pattern. Watch the steps I use:**

1. **I find the vowel letter by pointing to it. There is 1 vowel letter followed by 1 or more consonants.**

2. **The syllable type is closed and the gesture looks like this.** 
   (Gesture and say "closed.")

3. **Next, I look to see if there is a 3-letter blend before the vowel. There are 3 consonants, *s-p-r*, side by side before the vowel.**

4. **This word HAS the 3-letter blend pattern.**

5. **I place the word in the 3-letter blends column.**
   (Don't read the word yet.)

Let's sort the next word together. I'll answer and gesture with you.
(Display print.)

- **Look at this word. What do I do first?** **find the vowel letter**
  - **Yes, let's pretend to touch the vowel letter.**

- **How many vowel letters?** **1** **Is it followed by 1 or more consonants?** **yes**

- **Syllable type?**  **closed** **How do we know?** **1 vowel followed by 1 or more consonants**

- **Vowel sound?** **/ĭ/**

- **Are there 3 consonants side by side before the vowel?** **no**

- **Where does this word go?** **in the NO column**

| 3-Letter Blends | NO |
|---|---|
| sprint | print |

**Day 6**

Now it's your turn. Turn to page 11 in your Student Workbook. Decide if each word has an initial 3-letter blend. Then, write it in the correct column. Finally, read all the words in each column.

## Answer Key

| 3-Letter Blends | NO |
|---|---|
| sprint | print |
| strip | trip |
| scrub | rub |
| strap | traps |
| scrap | rap |
| split | slit |
| strand | stand |

**Routine for Word Sorting:**

- Find the vowel or vowels.
- How many vowel letters?
- Is it followed by 1 or more consonants?
- Syllable type gesture?
- Vowel sound?
- Is there an initial 3-letter blend?
- Where does this word go?
- Read the words.

| | |
|---|---|
| 1. strip | 7. strap |
| 2. scrub | 8. scrap |
| 3. trip | 9. split |
| 4. rub | 10. slit |
| 5. traps | 11. strand |
| 6. rap | 12. stand |

## Writing

### SOUND-SPELLING MAPPING WITH STUDENT PHONICS CHIPS

Today we're going to practice moving sound chips into boxes and then writing the letters to spell the words. Before we begin, let's review what the colors of the chips represent.

Repeat after me.

- The blue chips are for consonant sounds. The blue chips are for consonant sounds.
- The red chip is for short vowel sounds. The red chip is for short vowel sounds.

Let's do one together. Watch me move the chips and write the letters.

The first word is scram. Word? scram

Chips

- Finger-stretch scram. /s/ /k/ /r/ /ă/ /m/
- How many sounds? 5 How many boxes should I dot? 5
- First sound? /s/ Chip? blue
- Second sound? /k/ Chip? blue
- Third sound? /r/ Chip? blue
- Fourth sound? /ă/ Chip? red
- Last sound? /m/ Chip? blue
- Are there 3 consonants before the vowel? yes (Count the 3 blue chips before the red chip.)
- Sounds? /s/ /k/ /r/ /ă /m/
- Word? scram

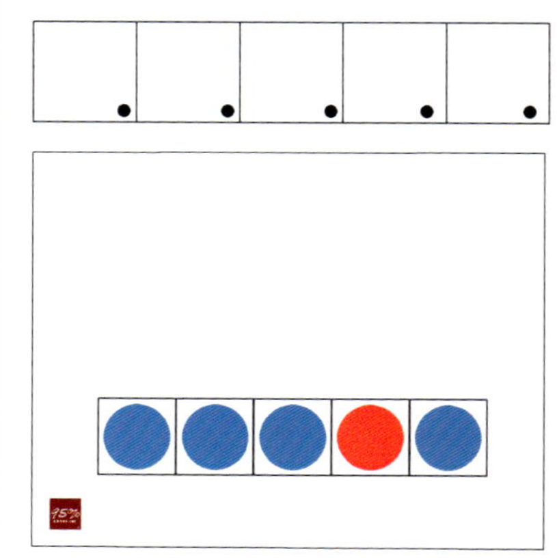

## Letters

- **Which letter spells the /s/ sound?** s
- **Which letter spells the /k/ sound?** c
- **Which letter spells the /r/ sound?** r
- **Which letter spells the /ă/ sound?** a
- **Which letter spells the /m/ sound?** m
- **Which letters spell the 3-letter blend?** s-c-r
- **Syllable type and gesture?** closed
- **Sounds?** /s/ /k/ /r/ /ă/ /m/
- **Word?** scram

Now it's your turn. Get your chips and mat ready. Remember to place the blue consonant chips on the left side, and the red vowel chip on the right side. Lay out the following chips on your mat:

- 4 blue chips
- 1 red chip

**Does your mat look like this?**

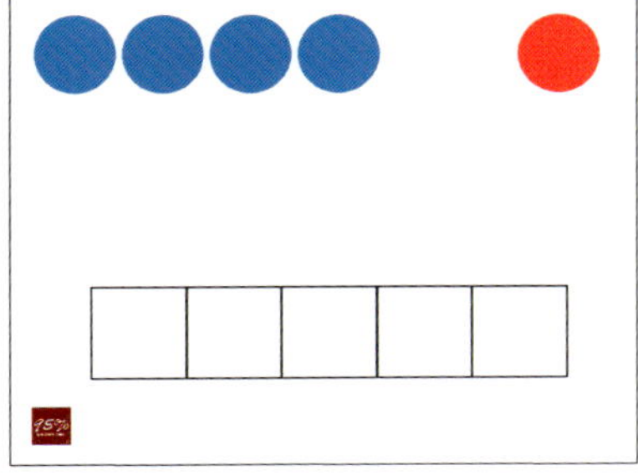

 **Turn to page 11 in your Student Workbook. Here are the steps:**

1. I'm going to say a word and you'll repeat it.
2. Finger-stretch the sounds and place dots in your workbook.
3. Then, move chips on your mat.
4. Write the letters in your workbook.
5. Finally, whisper read the word.

## Answer Key

| Words to Dictate | Placement of Phonics Chips on Mat | Correct Answers in Student Workbook |
|---|---|---|
| scram | 🔵🔵🔵🔴🔵 | s c r a m |
| 1. rust | 🔵🔴🔵🔵 | r u s t |
| 2. strip | 🔵🔵🔵🔴🔵 | s t r i p |
| 3. scrub | 🔵🔵🔵🔴🔵 | s c r u b |
| 4. stand | 🔵🔵🔴🔵🔵 | s t a n d |
| 5. split | 🔵🔵🔵🔴🔵 | s p l i t |

🔑 **Routine for Chip Movement:**

- **Finger-stretch sounds.**
  - **How many sounds?**
  - **How many boxes?**
  - **Dot boxes in workbook.**
- **Sound? Chip?** (repeat for each sound)
- **Which letter spells the /_/ sound?** (repeat for each sound)
- **Word?**

**Day 6**

## Passage Reading

### UNDERLINE PATTERN WORDS

### Passage – Literary: *Mud Splat!*

Now we'll practice finding initial 3-letter blend words in a passage. Our passage today is about having fun scrapping in mud. Mud scrapping is like painting but with mud. Have you ever played in mud?

Today we are going to look for closed syllable words that have the initial 3-letter blend pattern and underline them.

**Let's look at the title of the passage.** (Do not read the title.) **The word** *Splat* **follows the 3-letter blend pattern, so I make the closed syllable gesture and underline it. Help me find more words to underline. Hold up the closed syllable gesture when you see a word with the initial 3-letter blend, and I'll underline it.** (Continue underlining the initial 3-letter blend words above the black line.)

 Now it's your turn. Turn to page 12 in your Student Workbook. Here are the steps:

1. Begin at the black line and continue to the end of the passage.
2. Use your finger to find the vowel.
3. If you find an initial 3-letter blend word, underline it.
4. Finally, whisper read the words you underlined.

I'll give you a few minutes and we'll check them together.

## DAY 7

## Phonological Awareness Warm-Up

Today we are going to practice <u>phoneme segmentation</u>. Let's review the instructions:

- I'll say a word and you repeat it.
- Then, tell me the sounds in the word. Ready?

| Say tree: (**tree**) Sounds? | /t/ /r/ /ē/ | Say scat: (**scat**) Sounds? | /s/ /k/ /ă/ /t/ |
| Say shock: (**shock**) Sounds? | /sh/ /ŏ/ /k/ | Say champ: (**champ**) Sounds? | /ch/ /ă/ /m/ /p/ |
| Say treat: (**treat**) Sounds? | /t/ /r/ /ē/ /t/ | Say green: (**green**) Sounds? | /g/ /r/ /ē/ /n/ |
| Say shack: (**shack**) Sounds? | /sh/ /ă/ /k/ | Say scrap: (**scrap**) Sounds? | /s/ /k/ /r/ /ă/ /p/ |
| Say flip: (**flip**) Sounds? | /f/ /l/ /ĭ/ /p/ | Say braid: (**braid**) Sounds? | /b/ /r/ /ā/ /d/ |
| Say ramp: (**ramp**) Sounds? | /r/ /ă/ /m/ /p/ | Say chip: (**chip**) Sounds? | /ch/ /ĭ/ /p/ |
| Say sharp: (**sharp**) Sounds? | /sh/ /ar/ /p/ | Say class: (**class**) Sounds? | /k/ /l/ /ă/ /s/ |
| Say flash: (**flash**) Sounds? | /f/ /l/ /ă/ /sh/ | Say sand: (**sand**) Sounds? | /s/ /ă/ /n/ /d/ |

## Phonics Pattern

### READING PATTERN WORDS

### Review the Pattern

We're continuing to read and spell words with an initial 3-letter blend.

Let's review.

Does the word *initial* mean at the beginning or at the end? at the beginning

Repeat after me: An initial 3-letter blend has 3 consonants side by side before the vowel. Each consonant in a blend is pronounced.

Now, let's review the closed syllable pattern. Say it with me: Closed syllable words have 1 vowel letter followed by 1 or more consonants, and the vowel sound is short.

The gesture for the closed syllable is a closed fist.

Practice the gesture with me. 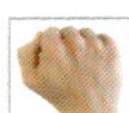 closed

### Read Pattern Words

Today we're going to read words with an initial 3-letter blend.

When I show you a word, follow these steps:
1. Find the vowel or vowels and say the number of vowel letters.
2. If the vowel is followed by 1 or more consonants, say "yes." Say "no" if it is not.
3. Say the syllable type and show the gesture.
4. Say the vowel sound.
5. Say "3-letter blend," if there is one. Say "no" if there is not a 3-letter blend.
6. Read the word.

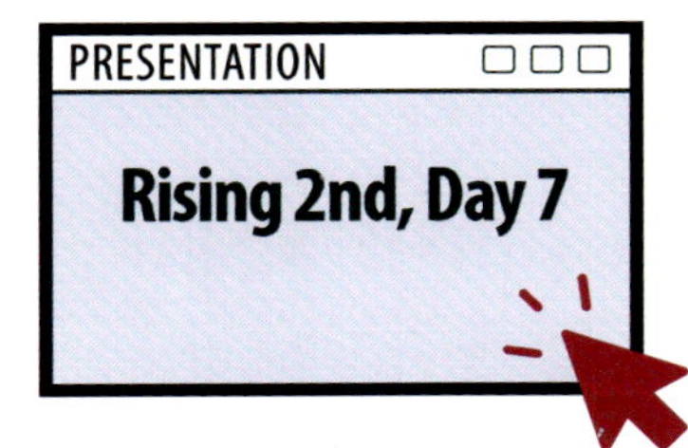


**Routine for Word Reading:**
- Find the vowel or vowels.
- How many vowel letters?
- Is it followed by 1 or more consonants?
- Syllable type and gesture?
- Vowel sound?
- Is there an initial 3-letter blend?
- Word?

## Answer Key

| Words on Presentation |
| --- |
| 1. (1, yes, closed, /ă/, 3-letter blend) - splat |
| 2. (1, yes, closed, /ă/, 3-letter blend) - scrap |
| 3. (1, yes, closed, /ĭ/, 3-letter blend) - sprint |
| 4. (1, yes, closed, /ă/, 3-letter blend) - strand |
| 5. (1, yes, closed, /ŏ/, no) - stop |
| 6. (1, yes, closed, /ĕ/, no) - spent |
| 7. (1, yes, closed, /ŭ/, 3-letter blend) - strut |
| 8. (1, yes, closed, /ĭ/, 3-letter blend) - script |
| 9. (1, yes, closed, /ĭ/, 3-letter blend) - splint |
| 10. (1, yes, closed, /ŭ/, 3-letter blend) - scrub |

| |
| --- |
| 1. splat |
| 2. scrap |
| 3. sprint |
| 4. strand |
| 5. stop |
| 6. spent |
| 7. strut |
| 8. script |
| 9. splint |
| 10. scrub |

## Phonics Pattern

### SORT WORDS

Let's practice identifying words that fit the pattern and words that do not.

Watch what I do.

**The first word is <u>strut</u>.**
(Display strut.)

- First, I find the vowel and identify the syllable type.
- I see 1 vowel letter, *u*, followed by 1 or more consonants. This word follows the closed syllable pattern.
- I whisper "closed" while making the closed syllable gesture.
- Then, I whisper the vowel sound /ŭ/.
- Next, I look for an initial 3-letter blend. I see 3 consonants, *s-t-r*, before the vowel.
- This word HAS an initial 3-letter blend pattern.
- I place the word *strut* in the 3-letter blends column.
- Finally, I slide a finger under the word and whisper "strut."

| 3-Letter Blends |
| --- |

Now it's your turn. Turn to page 13 in your Student Workbook. Let's review the steps.

1. Look at the word to decide if it follows the closed syllable pattern.
2. Whisper the syllable type and gesture.
3. Whisper the vowel sound.
4. Look for an initial 3-letter blend.
5. Write the word in the correct column.
6. Finally whisper read all the words in each column.

I'll check back with you in a few minutes and then you can check your answers.

**Answer Key**

| 3-Letter Blends | NO |
|---|---|
| strut | stunt |
| scrub | rub |
| scrimp | crimp |
| split | lit |
| scram | crams |
| sprig | rig |

**Routine for Word Sorting:**
- Find the vowel or vowels.
- How many vowel letters?
- Is it followed by 1 or more consonants?
- Syllable type gesture?
- Vowel sound?
- Is there an initial 3-letter blend?
- Where does this word go?
- Read the words.

1. rub
2. crimp
3. lit
4. scrub
5. scrimp
6. crams
7. split
8. scram
9. rig
10. sprig

## Writing

### SOUND-SPELLING MAPPING

Now we're going to spell words with an initial 3-letter blend. Watch how I use the Sound-Spelling Mapping paper. Each box holds only 1 sound.

The word is split.
- First, I finger-stretch and say the sounds: /s/ /p/ /l/ /ĭ/ /t/ – 5 sounds
- I need 5 boxes. I tap and mark a dot in the bottom right corner for each sound I hear: /s/ /p/ /l/ /ĭ/ /t/.
- Now, I write the letters that represent each sound.
  - The first sound is /s/. I write the letter *s* in the first box.
  - The second sound is /p/. I write the letter *p* in the second box.
  - The third sound is /l/. I write the letter *l* in the third box.
  - The fourth sound is /ĭ/. I write the letter *i* in the fourth box.
  - The last sound is /t/. I write the letter *t* in the last box.

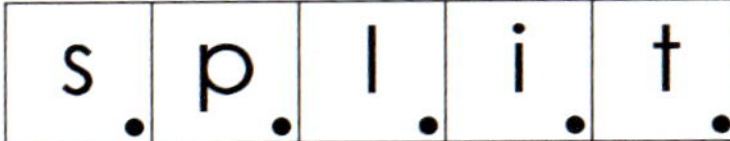

- **The syllable type is closed.** (Make the closed gesture under the word.)
- **There is an initial 3-letter blend, *s-p-l*.**
- **The sounds are /s/ /p/ /l/ /ĭ/ /t/.** (Touch under each letter.)
- **The word is split.** (Slide your finger under the word.)

**Let's try the next word together. The word is <u>sprig</u>. Word? sprig**
- **Finger-stretch and say the sounds.** /s/ /p/ /r/ /ĭ/ /g/
- **How many sounds?** 5 **How many boxes?** 5
- **We need 5 boxes. We tap and mark a dot in the bottom right corner for each sound.** /s/ /p/ /r/ /ĭ/ /g/
- **Now we write the letters.**
  - **Which letter spells the /s/ sound?** s **Which box?** first
  - **Which letter spells the /p/ sound?** p **Which box?** second
  - **Which letter spells the /r/ sound?** r **Which box?** third
  - **Which letter spells the /ĭ/ sound?** i **Which box?** fourth
  - **Which letter spells the /g/ sound?** g **Which box?** fifth
- **Is there an initial 3-letter blend?** yes
- **Syllable type and gesture?** closed
- **Sounds?** /s/ /p/ /r/ /ĭ/ /g/
- **Word?** sprig

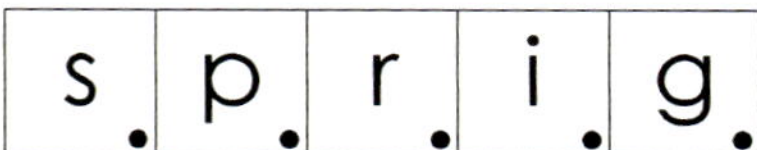

 **Now it's your turn. Turn to page 13 in your Student Workbook. Here are the steps:**

1. **Finger-stretch while saying the sounds.**
2. **Count the sounds.**
3. **Place a dot in the bottom right corner of the boxes you'll need.**
4. **Write the letters. Remember that each sound gets its own box.**
5. **Look for an initial 3-letter blend.**
6. **Whisper the syllable type and read the word to yourself.**

**Answer Key**

| Words to Dictate | Correct Answers in Student Workbook |
|---|---|
| sprig | s p r i g |
| 1. splat | s p l a t |
| 2. stop | s t o p |
| 3. crimp | c r i m p |
| 4. strum | s t r u m |
| 5. scrap | s c r a p |

## Passage Reading

### READ PASSAGE

**Passage – Literary: *Mud Splat!***

Now we'll read the passage we underlined yesterday. This passage is about a kid who fell and was covered in mud. Have you ever been muddy?

First, we'll read some of the underlined words together. When you see the initial 3-letter blend in the underlined words, make the closed syllable gesture and read the word. What is the underlined word in the title? **splat** Read with me just the underlined words above the black line.

Now it's your turn. Turn to page 12 in your Student Workbook. Here are the steps:

1. First, whisper read all the underlined words in the rest of the passage.
2. Then, go back to the beginning and whisper read the passage.

## Comprehension

### WRITTEN RESPONSE

Turn to page 13 in your Student Workbook. Complete the sentence about the passage. I'll give you a minute to do this, and then I'll ask for a couple of students to share what they wrote.

**Mom asked the kid to get ___________.** **(RL.1.1)**  (the tub with the straps)

 **Teacher Tip**

How are your students doing on the sound-spelling mapping? While the phonics chips take some classroom management time, having students move the chips is well worth it. You may wish to have each student store the individual manipulatives kit in a plastic zippered bag at his/her desk or cubicle.

Day
8

# DAY 8

## Phonological Awareness Warm-Up

**Today we are going to practice <u>phoneme segmentation</u>. Let's review the instructions:**

- **I'll say a word and you repeat it.**
- **Then, tell me the sounds in the word. Ready?**

| | | | |
|---|---|---|---|
| Say shop: (shop) Sounds? | /sh/ /ŏ/ /p/ | Say clock: (clock) Sounds? | /k/ /l/ /ŏ/ /k/ |
| Say swim: (swim) Sounds? | /s/ /w/ /ĭ/ /m/ | Say most: (most) Sounds? | /m/ /ō/ /s/ /t/ |
| Say great: (great) Sounds? | /g/ /r/ /ā/ /t/ | Say plop: (plop) Sounds? | /p/ /l/ /ŏ/ /p/ |
| Say with: (with) Sounds? | /w/ /ĭ/ /th/ | Say jump: (jump) Sounds? | /j/ /ŭ/ /m/ /p/ |
| Say plate: (plate) Sounds? | /p/ /l/ /ā/ /t/ | Say snap: (snap) Sounds? | /s/ /n/ /ă/ /p/ |
| Say coast: (coast) Sounds? | /k/ /ō/ /s/ /t/ | Say miss: (miss) Sounds? | /m/ /ĭ/ /s/ |
| Say sharp: (sharp) Sounds? | /sh/ /ar/ /p/ | Say stop: (stop) Sounds? | /s/ /t/ /ŏ/ /p/ |
| Say smash: (smash) Sounds? | /s/ /m/ /ă/ /sh/ | Say dive: (dive) Sounds? | /d/ /ī/ /v/ |

 **Teacher Tip**

Notice if students have more difficulty segmenting 4-phoneme words compared to when there are only 3 phonemes. If they struggle, you may wish to devote additional time to practicing phoneme segmentation because this is a skill that should have been mastered by late kindergarten.

## Phonics Pattern

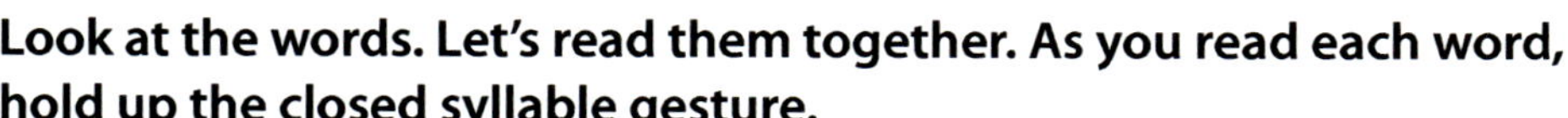

### WORD READING ACCURACY

**Look at the words. Let's read them together. As you read each word, hold up the closed syllable gesture.**

| | | | |
|---|---|---|---|
| rub | split | script | scram |
| strand | stop | sprint | lint |
| spot | cram | strip | strut |
| print | strap | strum | strict |
| scrap | splint | scrub | splat |

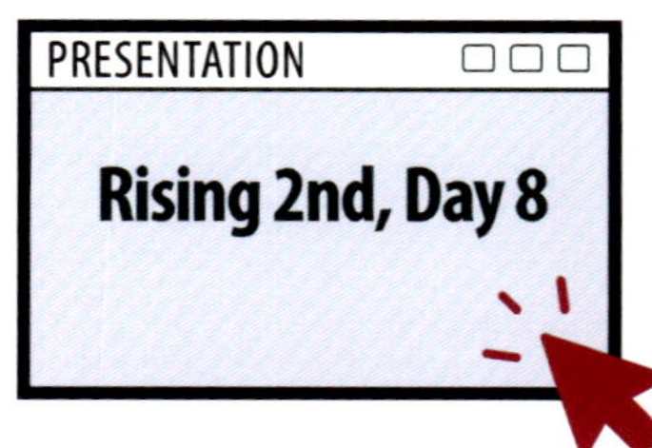

## Writing

### SOUND-SPELLING MAPPING WITH STUDENT PHONICS CHIPS

Today we're going to practice moving sound chips into boxes and then writing the letters to spell the words.

**Let's do one together. Watch me move the chips and write the letters.**

**The first word is** <u>scrap</u>**. Word?** scrap

**Chips**
- **Finger-stretch scrap.** /s/ /k/ /r/ /ă/ /p/
- **How many sounds?** 5 **How many boxes should I dot?** 5
- **First sound?** /s/ **Chip?** blue
- **Second sound?** /k/ **Chip?** blue
- **Third sound?** /r/ **Chip?** blue
- **Fourth sound?** /ă/ **Chip?** red
- **Last sound?** /p/ **Chip?** blue
- **Are there 3 consonants before the vowel?** yes (Count the 3 blue chips before the red chip.)
- **Sounds?** /s/ /k/ /r/ /ă/ /p/
- **Word?** scrap

**Letters**
- **Which letter spells the /s/ sound?** s
- **Which letter spells the /k/ sound?** c
- **Which letter spells the /r/ sound?** r
- **Which letter spells the /ă/ sound?** a
- **Which letter spells the /p/ sound?** p
- **Which letters spell the 3-letter blend?** s-c-r
- **Syllable type and gesture?** closed
- **Sounds?** /s/ /k/ /r/ /ă/ /p/
- **Word?** scrap

Now it's your turn. Get your chips and mat ready. Remember to place the blue consonant chips on the left side, and the red short vowel chip on the right side. Lay out the following chips on your mat:
- 4 blue chips
- 1 red chip

Does your mat look like this?

**What type of sound do the blue chips represent?** consonant
**What type of sound does the red chip represent?** short vowel

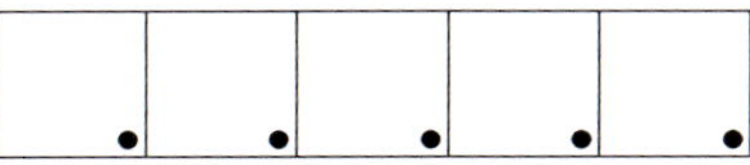

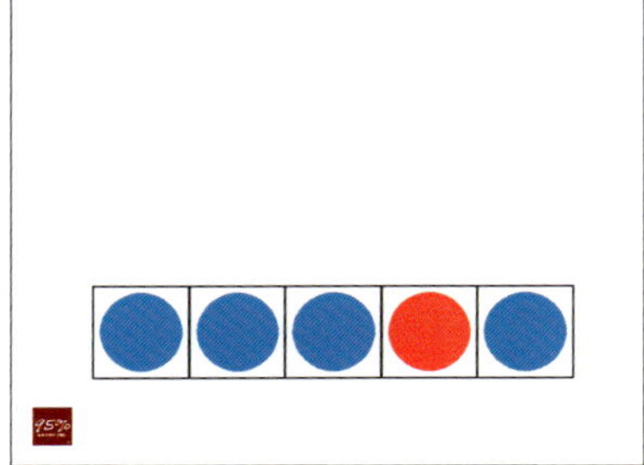

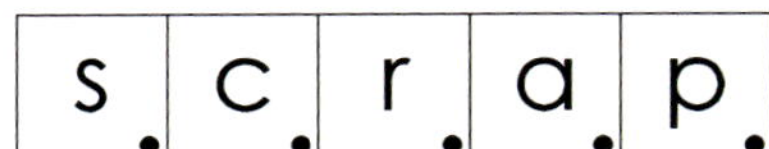


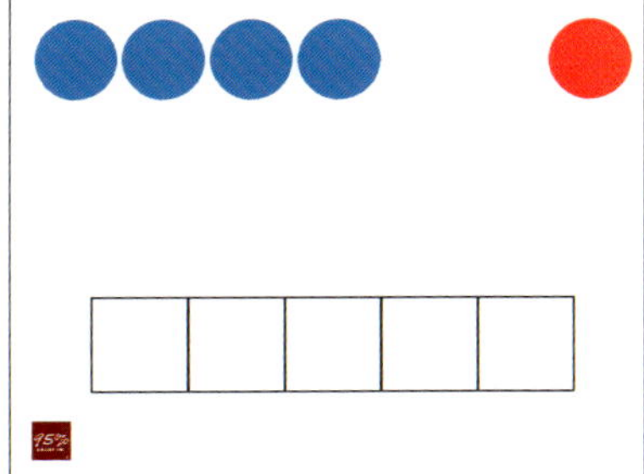

**Day 8**

 **Turn to page 14 in your Student Workbook. Here are the steps:**

1. I'm going to say a word and you'll repeat it.
2. Finger-stretch the sounds and place dots in your workbook.
3. Then, move chips on your mat.
4. Write the letters in your workbook.
5. Finally, whisper read the word.

**Answer Key**

| Words to Dictate | Placement of Phonics Chips on Mat | Correct Answers in Student Workbook |
|---|---|---|
| scrap | 🔵🔵🔵🔴🔵 | s c r a p |
| 1. split | 🔵🔵🔵🔴🔵 | s p l i t |
| 2. rests | 🔵🔴🔵🔵🔵 | r e s t s |
| 3. scrub | 🔵🔵🔵🔴🔵 | s c r u b |
| 4. strut | 🔵🔵🔵🔴🔵 | s t r u t |
| 5. print | 🔵🔵🔴🔵🔵 | p r i n t |

**🔑 Routine for Chip Movement:**

- **Finger-stretch sounds.**
  – How many sounds?
  – How many boxes?
  – Dot boxes in workbook.
- **Sound? Chip?** (repeat for each sound)
- **Which letter spells the /_/ sound?** (repeat for each sound)
- **Word?**

## Passage Reading

### UNDERLINE PATTERN WORDS

**Passage – Informational: *Scrub the Mud Out***

Now it's time to practice with a new passage. This passage is about getting mud out of clothes. Mud stains can be difficult to remove.

We'll underline only closed syllable words with the initial 3-letter blend pattern. Let's begin with the title. Which is the first word to underline? **scrub**

Help me find more 3-letter blends. If you see a word with an initial 3-letter blend, hold up the closed syllable gesture and I'll underline it. (Continue underlining the 3-letter blend words to the black line.)

 **Now it's your turn. Turn to page 14 in your Student Workbook. Here are the steps:**

1. Begin below the black line where none of the words are underlined.
2. Look at each word and point to the vowel.
3. If the word has an initial 3-letter blend, underline it.
4. Finally, whisper read the words you underlined.

I'll give you a few minutes to continue underlining through the end of the passage and then we'll check them together.

Day
**9**

# DAY 9

## Phonological Awareness Warm-Up

Today we are going to practice <u>phoneme segmentation</u>. Let's review the instructions:
- I'll say a word and you repeat it.
- Then, tell me the sounds in the word. Ready?

| | | | |
|---|---|---|---|
| Say sun: (**sun**) Sounds? | /s/ /ŭ/ /n/ | Say fly: (**fly**) Sounds? | /f/ /l/ /ī/ |
| Say soft: (**soft**) Sounds? | /s/ /ŏ/ /f/ /t/ | Say clay: (**clay**) Sounds? | /k/ /l/ /ā/ |
| Say drive: (**drive**) Sounds? | /d/ /r/ /ī/ /v/ | Say block: (**block**) Sounds? | /b/ /l/ /ŏ/ /k/ |
| Say charm: (**charm**) Sounds? | /ch/ /ar/ /m/ | Say spoke: (**spoke**) Sounds? | /s/ /p/ /ō/ /k/ |
| Say chow: (**chow**) Sounds? | /ch/ /ou/ | Say slim: (**slim**) Sounds? | /s/ /l/ /ĭ/ /m/ |
| Say safe: (**safe**) Sounds? | /s/ /ā/ /f/ | Say crack: (**crack**) Sounds? | /k/ /r/ /ă/ /k/ |
| Say turn: (**turn**) Sounds? | /t/ /er/ /n/ | Say mouse: (**mouse**) Sounds? | /m/ /ou/ /s/ |
| Say smell: (**smell**) Sounds? | /s/ /m/ /ĕ/ /l/ | Say seat: (**seat**) Sounds? | /s/ /ē/ /t/ |

## Fluency

### HIGH-FREQUENCY WORDS

Display the high-frequency word grid. Prompt students by saying **"Word?"** at each box.

| how | know | from | any |
|---|---|---|---|
| over | just | ask | an |
| were | them | could | when |
| where | that | little | jump |

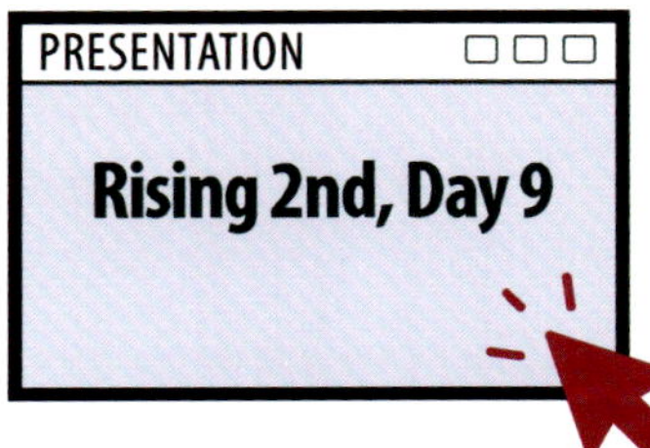


**Now it's your turn. Turn to page 15 in your Student Workbook. When I say "begin," tap under the first word and whisper read it. Read across the rows until I say "stop." Circle the last word you read. If you finish before I say "stop," go up to the top and read the words again.** (Time students for 1 minute. Say "stop" and ask students to circle the last word that was read.)

| over | were | ask | from |
|---|---|---|---|
| when | just | that | could |
| an | jump | how | little |
| know | them | where | any |

 

Day 9

## Writing

### WORD CHAINS

It's word chain time! We've done this before. Remember how we begin with 1 word and then spell others in a chain? We'll add, delete, or change 1 sound at a time to spell a new word.

Let's do this first one together.

The first word is <u>strap</u>.

Let's change <u>strap</u> to <u>trap</u>.
- **Which sound changes?** delete /s/ from the beginning
- **Which letter changes?** delete the letter *s* from the beginning

I write the word *trap* under *strap*.

Next, let's change <u>trap</u> to <u>trip</u>.
- **Which sound changes?** /ă/ changes to /ĭ/
- **Which letter changes?** change the letter *a* to *i*

I write the word *trip* under *trap*.

Finally, let's change <u>trip</u> to <u>strip</u>.
- **Which sound changes?** add /s/ to the beginning
- **Which letter changes?** add the letter *s* to the beginning

I write the word *strip* under *trip*.

Now it's your turn. Turn to page 15 in your Student Workbook. You'll find a spot to write 4 word chains. I'll tell you 1 word at a time and you'll write each new word below the old one. Find the page and look up when you're ready.

| strap |
|-------|
| trap |
| trip |
| strip |

***Note:*** If you are writing the words on the board, make sure you build the words going down, not across.

**Routine for Word Chains:**

- Change word *x* to word *y*.
  – Which sound changes?
  – Which letter(s) changes?
- Write word *y* under word *x*.

### Answer Key

| splint | grass | slop | scram |
|--------|-------|------|-------|
| split | brass | stop | cram |
| splat | bran | step | ram |
| spat | brand | strep | tram |

Day
9

## Passage Reading

### READ PASSAGE

#### Passage – Informational: *Scrub the Mud Out*

Now it's time to read a passage. Our passage is about how to get out mud stains. Have you had stains on your clothes that wouldn't come out?

First, we'll read some of the underlined words together. When you see the initial 3-letter blend in the underlined words, make the closed syllable gesture and read the word. What is the underlined word in the title? scrub Read with me just the underlined words above the black line.

Now it's your turn. Turn to page 14 in your Student Workbook. Here are the steps:

1. First, whisper read all the underlined words in the rest of the passage.
2. Then, go back to the beginning and whisper read the passage.

## Comprehension

### ORAL RESPONSE

Now that you've read the passage, let's talk about it.
- **What is the main topic of this passage?  (RI.1.2)** (how to get mud splats out of pants)
- **"Grab the pants and strap them up." What is "strap up"? (RI.1.4)** (hang them up)

# DAY 10

## Phonological Awareness Warm-Up

Today we are going to practice <u>phoneme segmentation</u>. Let's review the instructions:
- **I'll say a word and you repeat it.**
- **Then, tell me the sounds in the word. Ready?**

| | | | |
|---|---|---|---|
| Say phone: (**phone**) Sounds? | /f/ /ō/ /n/ | Say plan: (**plan**) Sounds? | /p/ /l/ /ă/ /n/ |
| Say sled: (**sled**) Sounds? | /s/ /l/ /ĕ/ /d/ | Say lift: (**lift**) Sounds? | /l/ /ĭ/ /f/ /t/ |
| Say skip: (**skip**) Sounds? | /s/ /k/ /ĭ/ /p/ | Say time: (**time**) Sounds? | /t/ /ī/ /m/ |
| Say chime: (**chime**) Sounds? | /ch/ /ī/ /m/ | Say rope: (**rope**) Sounds? | /r/ /ō/ /p/ |
| Say late: (**late**) Sounds? | /l/ /ā/ /t/ | Say game: (**game**) Sounds? | /g/ /ā/ /m/ |
| Say hope: (**hope**) Sounds? | /h/ /ō/ /p/ | Say spin: (**spin**) Sounds? | /s/ /p/ /ĭ/ /n/ |
| Say it: (**it**) Sounds? | /ĭ/ /t/ | Say rock: (**rock**) Sounds? | /r/ /ŏ/ /k/ |
| Say crash: (**crash**) Sounds? | /k/ /r/ /ă/ /sh/ | Say rust: (**rust**) Sounds? | /r/ /ŭ/ /s/ /t/ |

## High-Frequency Words

### NUMBER OF SOUNDS IN HIGH-FREQUENCY WORDS

Today we are working with high-frequency words. We'll decide how many sounds are in each word and write it in the correct column. Let's do one together.

(Display <u>how</u>.)

**Here is the first word: <u>how</u>. Word? how**

- **Finger-stretch how. /h/ /ou/ How many sounds? 2**
- **I write the word *how* in the column labeled "2 Sounds."**
- **Say the sounds aloud as I write the letters. /h/ /ou/**
  - **Notice the word *how* is spelled with 3 letters, *h-o-w*, but there are only 2 sounds. The letters *o-w* make 1 sound, /ou/.**
- **Word? how**

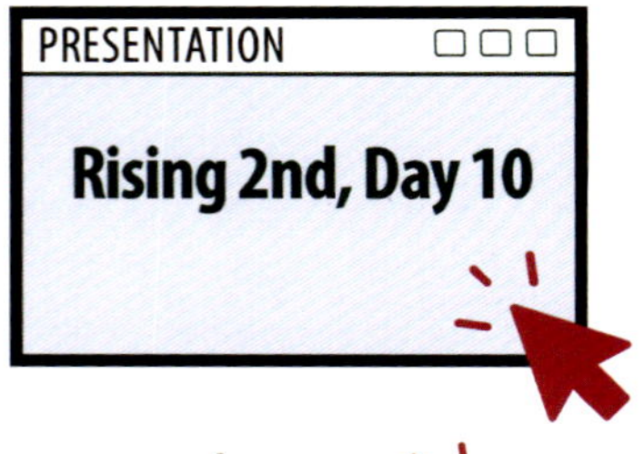


| 2 Sounds | 3 Sounds | 4 Sounds |
|---|---|---|
| how | | |

**Now it's your turn. Turn to page 16 in your Student Workbook. Look at the word list. For each word, follow these steps:**

1. **Read the word.**
2. **Finger-stretch and count the sounds.**
3. **Write the word in the correct column and say the sounds as you write the letters.**
4. **Read the word.**

## Answer Key

| 2 Sounds | 3 Sounds | 4 Sounds |
|---|---|---|
| how | but | funny |
| know | with | want |
| ate | ask | |
| they | | |

| | |
|---|---|
| 1. but | 5. want |
| 2. know | 6. they |
| 3. funny | 7. with |
| 4. ate | 8. ask |

*Note:* Students may need multiple reminders that they are sorting the words by number of sounds, not number of letters.

## Fluency

### WORDS

**We've been learning to read closed syllable words with the initial 3-letter blend pattern. Remember, the vowel sound is short in a closed syllable.**

**Look at this word grid. Please read it aloud chorally as a class. Ready?**

| scrub | strand | strut | splat |
|---|---|---|---|
| sprint | split | strum | scrap |

**Now it's your turn. Turn to page 16 in your Student Workbook. When I say "begin," point to the first word. Whisper read across the page. If you finish before I say "stop," start at the top and read the words again.** (Time students for 1 minute. Say "stop" and ask students to circle the last word that was read.)

| script | split | strand | splat |
|---|---|---|---|
| sprint | scrap | strep | strip |
| strum | strap | sprig | strut |
| scrub | splint | strict | scram |

### PHRASES

**Next we're going to read phrases. Let's practice 4 phrases all together.**

| scrub the tub | got a splint | splat on the mat | have a script |
|---|---|---|---|

**Now it's your turn. Turn to page 16 in your Student Workbook. When I say "begin," point to the first phrase and whisper it. Continue reading across the page. If you finish before I say "stop," start at the top and read the phrases again.** (Time students for 1 minute. Say "stop" and ask students to circle the last phrase that was read.)

| when he splits | in a sprint | splat on the mat | cut the sprig |
| --- | --- | --- | --- |
| split the strap | splint my leg | on a scrap | scrap the script |
| strum and hum | scrub the tub | strut on down | got a splint |
| have a script | scrub the step | a bit strict | get the strip |

## Writing

### SENTENCE DICTATION

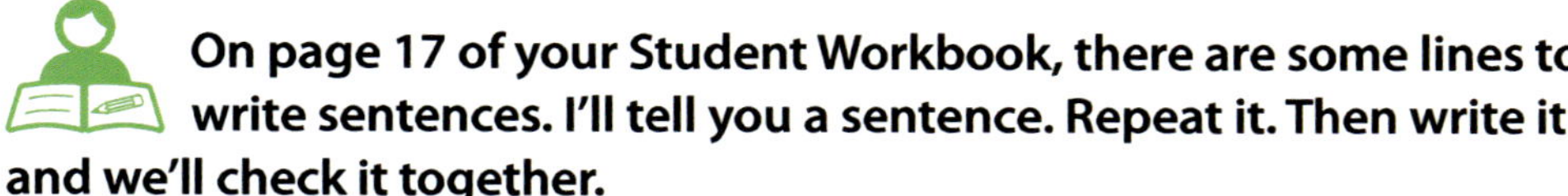

**On page 17 of your Student Workbook, there are some lines to write sentences. I'll tell you a sentence. Repeat it. Then write it and we'll check it together.**

**First sentence: They had to scrub the mud. Repeat it with me. Now write it.**

Now let's check it. Look at this sentence. Place a dot under each letter and punctuation mark if you got it right. Correct it if needed.

**Second sentence: I will sprint down the steps. Repeat it with me. Now write it.** (Repeat the correction procedure above.)

**Third sentence: Do not scrimp on the suds. Repeat it with me. Now write it.** (Repeat the correction procedure above.)

## Passage Reading

### READ PASSAGES

**Today you are going to practice reading both of the passages. One was about cleaning up after scrapping in mud. The second was about getting mud spots out of pants.**

## Comprehension

### WRITTEN RESPONSE

**Turn to page 17 in your Student Workbook. Read both passages, and then write the answer to the question for each passage in your workbook.**

**Passage – Literary:** *Mud Splat!* **on page 12**
  1. **"I was masked in mud splats." What is "masked"?  (RL.1.4)**
     (covered)

**Passage – Informational:** *Scrub the Mud Out* **on page 14**
  1. **"Do not scrimp on the suds." What is "scrimp"?  (RI.1.4)** (to use
     just a little)

---

 **Teacher Tip**

The process of asking students to look for pattern words and underline them helps reinforce a good habit in learning new words. It reminds students to study the letters left to right. Analyzing the letter strings in words is the most effective way to learn and remember words. The goal is for students to avoid ineffective cues like word shape or initial letter, but rather to develop fluency at recognizing common strings of letters in the interior of unfamiliar words.

---

     

# The Next Plan

1     I like to run up the hill on the rock <u>path</u> for fun. I go to the <u>path</u> to

2 get fit. I went as fast as I could up the hill <u>when</u> all of a (sudden) I tripped

3 and fell <u>with</u> a <u>thump</u>. I fell from a big rock at the end of the <u>path</u>. The skin

4 on my <u>shin</u> was cut and my leg felt as if it had snapped. <u>Then</u>, I limped to

5 the <u>bench</u>. <u>This</u> was not fun.

6     My mom <u>rushed</u> to get my leg looked at fast. I left <u>with</u> my hand in a

7 splint and my leg in a cast. I was asked to rest and not <u>dash</u> up any steps.

8 I asked my mom to get my <u>chest</u> of funny tricks. I had a plan. I prepped

9 all my tricks, <u>then</u> asked my pals to drop over. I grabbed a (rabbit) out of a

10 (velvet) hat and mocked my pals <u>with</u> tricks <u>that</u> left <u>them</u> stumped. I was

11 a <u>smash</u> hit! After I got rid of the cast, I wanted to find a new <u>path</u> to run.

12 <u>That</u> was my next plan.

**Note:** The word *the* is not a pattern word because it is not a closed syllable.

| Consonants Digraphs | | | | | Simple Closed Multisyllable | Word Count* |
|---|---|---|---|---|---|---|
| **ch** | **sh** | **th** | | **wh** | | 190 |
| bench | dash | path | with | when | rabbit | **Pattern Words** |
| chest | rush | that | | | sudden | 24 (13%) |
| | shin | them | | | velvet | * including title |
| | smash | then | | | | |
| | | this | | | | |
| | | thump | | | | |

 95 Phonics Booster Bundle™: Summer School Edition 2021 • Rising Second • Teacher's Edition 

## Passage – Informational

# Chipmunks

1     Chipmunks are little brown mammals. You can find them

2  in brush, shrubs, and grass. Chipmunks like to sprint and jump. They will sit

3  on a big branch and look over the land. They run if they see a spat.

4     Chipmunks have a lot of spunk. When they want to find a chipmunk

5  pal, they stand up on back legs. Then they chit, chit, chit with a shrill

6  and make a lot of rumpus. They chomp on nuts held in the front hands.

7  They spit the shells out so they can munch the pulp. When you look in a

8  chipmunk's nest, you will see a mess of shells.

9     They craft a new nest when they are still little. The nest is where

10  they rest and stash tidbits for when it chills. Chipmunks are not good pets.

11  They are best left out in the grass where they can run and jump as much

12  as they want.

**Note:** The words *the*, *they*, and *where* are not pattern words because they are not a closed syllable.

| Consonant Digraphs | | | | Simple Closed Multisyllable | Word Count* |
|---|---|---|---|---|---|
| **ch** | **sh** | **th** | **wh** | | 156 |
| branch | brush | that | when | chipmunk | **Pattern Words** |
| chill | shell | them | | mammal | 31 (20%) |
| chit | shrill | then | | rumpus | * including title |
| chomp | shrub | with | | tidbit | |
| munch | shun | | | | |
| | stash | | | | |

     95 Phonics Booster Bundle™: Summer School Edition 2021 • Rising Second • Teacher's Edition    **53**

**Day 11**

# Days 11–15: Consonant Digraphs ch, sh, th, wh

## Learning Objective

In Days 11–15, students demonstrate understanding of consonant digraphs in closed syllable words, as well as an understanding of simple multisyllable words, by correctly identifying, reading, and writing pattern words in isolation and in passages.

# DAY 11

## Phonological Awareness Warm-Up

Today we are going to practice <u>adding a sound to the beginning or end</u> of a word to make a new word.

**Watch me. My turn.**
- The word is <u>eel</u>. I add /s/ to the beginning of the word. The new word is <u>seal</u>.

**Now, I will add a sound to the end of a word. Watch me. My turn.**
- The word is <u>fee</u>. I add /t/ to the end of the word. The new word is <u>feet</u>.

**Let's practice a couple together.**
- **Say pie: (pie) Add /s/ to the beginning. Word?** spy
- **Say we: (we) Add /k/ to the end. Word?** week

**Now it's your turn. Here are the directions:**
- **I'll say a word and you repeat it.**
- **Next, I'll tell you what sound to add to the beginning or end of the word.**
- **Then, tell me the new word. Ready?**

| | | | | |
|---|---|---|---|---|
| Say talk: (talk) Add /s/ to the beginning. Word? | stalk | Say ten: (ten) Add /t/ to the end. Word? | tent |
| Say in: (in) Add /p/ to the beginning. Word? | pin | Say bun: (bun) Add /k/ to the end. Word? | bunk |
| Say elf: (elf) Add /sh/ to the beginning. Word? | shelf | Say far: (far) Add /m/ to the end. Word? | farm |
| Say at: (at) Add /ch/ to the beginning. Word? | chat | Say eye: (eye) Add /s/ to the end. Word? | ice |
| Say at: (at) Add /k/ to the beginning. Word? | cat | Say tray: (tray) Add /n/ to the end. Word? | train |
| Say lock: (lock) Add /b/ to the beginning. Word? | block | Say shoe: (shoe) Add /t/ to the end. Word? | shoot |
| Say eat: (eat) Add /f/ to the beginning. Word? | feet | Say flow: (flow) Add /t/ to the end. Word? | float |
| Say eye: (eye) Add /m/ to the beginning. Word? | my | Say hi: (hi) Add /k/ to the end. Word? | hike |

 95 Phonics Booster Bundle™: Summer School Edition 2021 • Rising Second • Teacher's Edition

Day
**11**

## Phonics Pattern

Today we are reviewing how to read and spell closed syllable words with the consonant digraphs *c-h*, *s-h*, *t-h*, or *w-h*. A consonant digraph has 1 sound spelled with 2 consonants side by side. The 2 consonants are pronounced as 1 sound.

Repeat it with me: A consonant digraph has 1 sound spelled with 2 consonants side by side.

Consonant digraphs *c-h*, *s-h*, and *t-h* can be found in the initial or final position of a word. Digraph *w-h* is only found in the initial position.

Let's review.
- Where is the initial position in a word? at the beginning
- Where is the final position in a word? at the end

The words in this lesson follow the closed syllable pattern. Let's review the pattern of a closed syllable.

Repeat it with me: Closed syllable words have 1 vowel letter followed by 1 or more consonants, and the vowel sound is short.

The gesture for a closed syllable is a closed fist.

Practice the gesture with me. 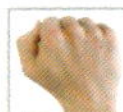

(Display positional keywords.)

Let's review the "positional keywords" for the consonant digraphs. As I show each one, say the keyword and then say the sound.

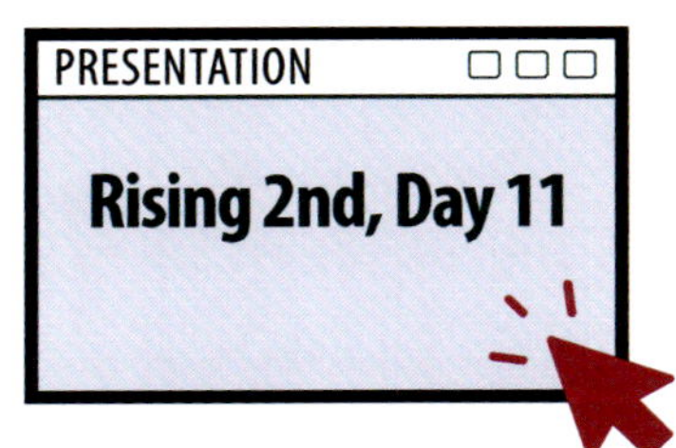


| Key Card | Positional Keyword |
|---|---|
| chair | chair<br>/ch/ at the beginning |
| bran<u>ch</u> | branch<br>/ch/ at the end |
| <u>sh</u>oe | shoe<br>/sh/ at the beginning |
| bru<u>sh</u> | brush<br>/sh/ at the end |
| <u>th</u>umb | thumb<br>/th/ at the beginning |
| mou<u>th</u> | mouth<br>/th/ at the end |
| <u>wh</u>ale | whale<br>/hw/ at the beginning |

*Note:* The digraph positional keywords cue students to attend to the digraph sounds in both initial and final positions.

*Note:* The sound for the digraph *wh* is called a glide because the sound glides immediately into the vowel. The sound is created as through it were /hw/, with a slight puff of air before /w/.

## SORT WORDS

(Display <u>bunch</u>.)

🔑 **I'm going to look for the c-h, s-h, t-h, or w-h consonant digraph patterns. Watch the steps I use:**

1. **I find the vowel letter by pointing to it. There is 1 vowel letter followed by 1 or more consonants.**

2. **The syllable type is closed and the gesture looks like this.** 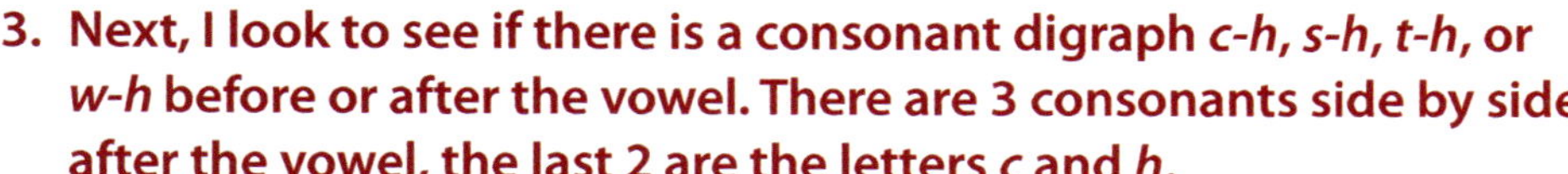

3. **Next, I look to see if there is a consonant digraph *c-h*, *s-h*, *t-h*, or *w-h* before or after the vowel. There are 3 consonants side by side after the vowel, the last 2 are the letters *c* and *h*.**

4. **This word HAS the consonant digraph *c-h* pattern in the final position.**

5. **I place the word in the final /ch/ branch column.** 
   (Don't read the word yet.)

(Display <u>bun</u>.)

**Let's sort the next word together. I'll answer and gesture with you.**

- **Look at this word. What do I do first? find the vowel letter**
  - **Yes, let's pretend to touch the vowel letter.**

- **How many vowel letters? 1**

- **Is the vowel followed by 1 or more consonants? yes**

- **Syllable type and gesture?**  **closed**

- **Vowel sound? /ŭ/**

- **Are there 2 consonants before or after the vowel letter? no**
  - **Does this word follow a c-h, s-h, t-h, or w-h consonant digraph pattern? no**

- **Where does this word go?** **in the NO column**

Now it's your turn. Turn to page 18 in your Student Workbook. Decide if each word has a c-h, s-h, t-h, or w-h consonant digraph pattern. Then, write the word in the correct column. Finally, read all the words in each column.

## Answer Key

| chair | bran<u>ch</u> | <u>sh</u>oe | bru<u>sh</u> |
|---|---|---|---|
| champ | bunch | shut | trash |
| chunk | rich | shelf | |

| <u>th</u>umb | mou<u>th</u> | <u>wh</u>ale | NO |
|---|---|---|---|
| that | cloth | whim | bun |
| thick | | whisk | camp |

**Routine for Word Sorting:**

- Find the vowel or vowels.
- How many vowel letters?
- Is there 1 or more consonants after the vowel?
- Syllable type gesture?
- Vowel sound?
- Is there a consonant digraph *c-h*, *s-h*, *t-h*, or *w-h*?
- Initial or final?
- Where does this word go?
- Read the words.

| | |
|---|---|
| 1. shut | 7. chunk |
| 2. champ | 8. trash |
| 3. that | 9. shelf |
| 4. whim | 10. rich |
| 5. whisk | 11. cloth |
| 6. camp | 12. thick |

## Writing

### SOUND-SPELLING MAPPING WITH STUDENT PHONICS CHIPS

Today we're going to practice moving sound chips into boxes and then writing the letters to spell the words. Today we have a new chip. The orange chip represents the single sound of a consonant digraph. It reminds us that, while it's spelled with 2 consonants, a digraph is pronounced as 1 sound.

Watch me, my turn.

The first word is <u>shrug</u>.

Chips

- First, I finger-stretch and say the sounds. /sh/ /r/ /ŭ/ /g/
- There are 4 sounds. I tap and place a dot in the bottom right corner of each box as I say the sounds. /sh/ /r/ /ŭ/ /g/
- Now, I move chips into the boxes to represent the sounds. Remember, blue chips are for consonant sounds, the red chip is for short vowel sounds, and the orange chip represents digraphs.
  - The first sound is /sh/. This is a consonant digraph so I pull down the orange chip.
  - The second sound is /r/. This a consonant sound so I pull down a blue chip.

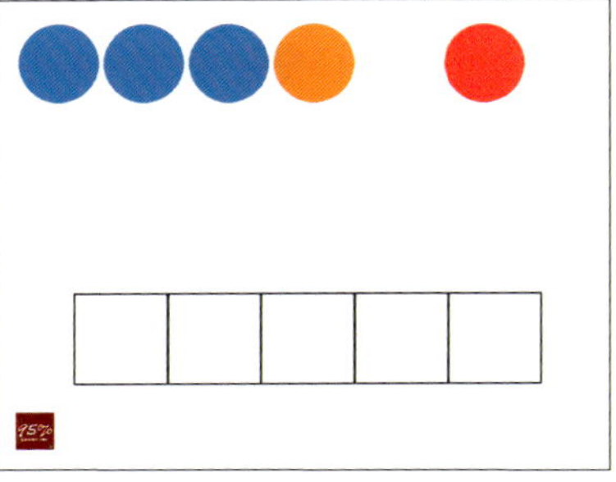
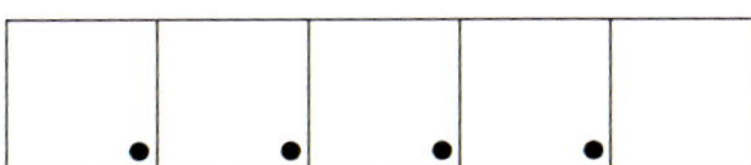

- – **The next sound is /ŭ/. This is a short vowel sound so I pull down the red chip.**
  - – **The last sound is /g/. This is a consonant sound so I pull down another blue chip.**
- **The sounds are /sh/ /r/ /ŭ/ /g/.** (Touch under each chip.)
- **The word is shrug.** (Slide your finger under the chips.)

**Letters**

- **Now, watch me write the letters that represent each sound.**
  - – **The /sh/ sound is spelled with the letters *s-h*, so I write them in the first box. Remember, the consonant digraph *sh* only gets 1 box because it makes 1 sound, /sh/.**
  - – **The second sound is /r/. I write the letter *r* in the second box.**
  - – **The third sound is /ŭ/. I write the letter *u* in the third box.**
  - – **The last sound is /g/. I write the letter *g* in the fourth box.**
- **The syllable type is closed.** (Model the closed gesture under the word.)
- **The sounds are /sh/ /r/ /ŭ/ /g/.** (Touch under each letter.)
- **The word is shrug.** (Slide your finger under the word.)

**Let's do one together. Watch me move the chips and write the letters.**

**The word is <u>tenth</u>. Word? tenth**

**Chips**

- **Finger-stretch tenth.** /t/ /ĕ/ /n/ /th/
- **How many sounds?** 4 **How many boxes should I dot?** 4
- **First sound?** /t/ **Chip?** blue
- **Second sound?** /ĕ/ **Chip?** red
- **Third sound?** /n/ **Chip?** blue
- **Last sound?** /th/ **Chip?** orange
  - – **Yes, the orange chip represents the digraph sound /th/.**
- **Sounds?** /t/ /ĕ/ /n/ /th/
- **Word?** tenth

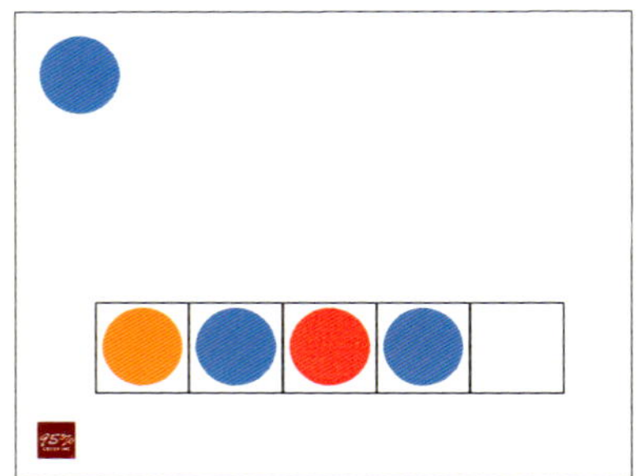

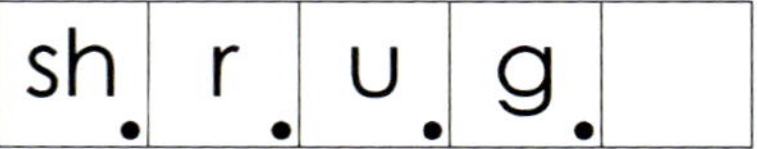

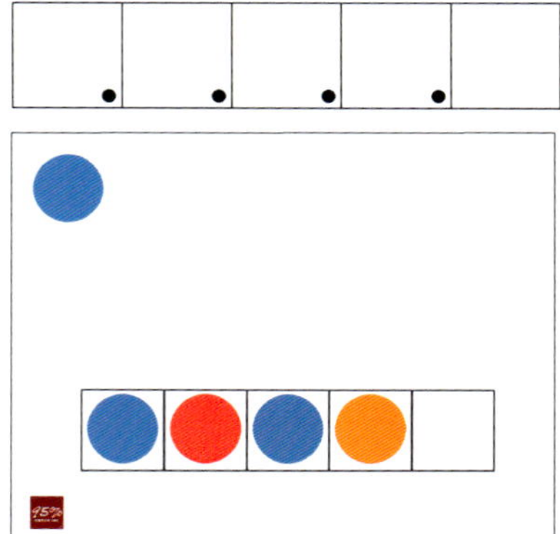

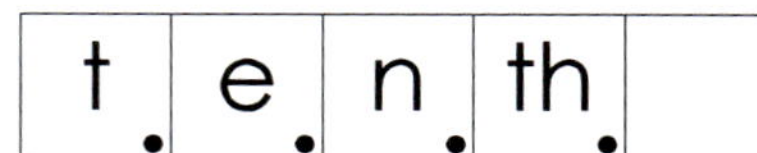

**Letters**

- **Which letter spells the /t/ sound?** t
- **Which letter spells the /ĕ/ sound?** e
- **Which letter spells the /n/ sound?** n
- **Which letter or letters spell the /th/ sound?** t-h
  - – **Since the consonant digraph *t-h* makes 1 sound, I write the letters *t-h* in 1 box.**
- **Syllable type and gesture?** closed **How do we know?** 1 vowel letter followed by 1 or more consonants
- **Sounds?** /t/ /ĕ/ /n/ /th/
- **Word?** tenth

 95 Phonics Booster Bundle™: Summer School Edition 2021 • Rising Second • Teacher's Edition

Now it's your turn. Get your chips and mat ready. Remember to place the blue consonant and orange consonant digraph chips on the left side, and the red vowel chip on the right side. Lay out the following chips on your mat:

- 3 blue chips
- 1 orange chip
- 1 red chip

**Does your mat look like this?**

**Turn to page 18 in your Student Workbook. Here are the steps:**

1. I'm going to say a word and you'll repeat it.
2. Finger-stretch the sounds and place dots in your workbook.
3. Then, move chips on your mat.
4. Write the letters in your workbook.
5. Finally, whisper read the word.

## Answer Key

| Words to Dictate | Placement of Phonics Chips on Mat | Correct Answers in Student Workbook |
|---|---|---|
| tenth | 🔵🔴🔵🟠 | t . e . n . th |
| 1. branch | 🔵🔵🔴🔵🟠 | b . r . a . n . ch |
| 2. cash | 🔵🔴🟠 | c . a . sh |
| 3. chimp | 🟠🔴🔵🔵 | ch . i . m . p |
| 4. trap | 🔵🔵🔴🔵 | t . r . a . p |
| 5. this | 🟠🔴🔵 | th . i . s |
| 6. grass | 🔵🔵🔴🔵 | g . r . a . ss |

*Note:* The double consonant *s* in the word *grass* (#6) follows the Floss Rule. The double consonant makes 1 sound but is not considered a digraph. Double consonants are represented by a blue chip.

**Routine for Chip Movement:**

- **Finger-stretch sounds.**
  - **How many sounds?**
  - **How many boxes?**
  - **Dot boxes in workbook.**
- **Sound? Chip?** (repeat for each sound)
- **Which letter spells the /_/ sound?** (repeat for each sound)
- **Word?**

## Writing

### POSSESSIVE NOUNS

Today we will learn about possessive nouns and how to write them. A noun is a person, place, or thing. A possessive noun shows that something belongs to the person, place, or thing. To show ownership, add an apostrophe and the letter *s*.

**Day 11**

**Watch what I do.**
(Display Tim has a pet cat. Tim___ cat is brown.)
- I read the sentences: Tim has a pet cat. Tim_ cat is brown.
- To show that Tim owns (or possesses) the cat, I place an apostrophe-s after his name in the second sentence, *Tim's cat is brown.*
- I write <u>Tim's cat</u> in the possessive noun column because the cat belongs to Tim.

 **Let's try some together. Turn to page 19 in your Student Workbook.**

(Display The cat___ toys are in the red bin.)
- Read the sentence with me. **The cat_ toys are in the red bin.**
- Whose toys are in the red bin? **the cat's**
- What do we need to add? **an apostrophe-s after the letter *t* in cat**
- Write <u>cat's toys</u> in the possessive noun column because the toys belong to the cat.

**Let's try one more.**
- If Mom has some flowers, what do we need to add to show Mom owns or possesses the flowers? **an apostrophe-s after the second letter *m* in Mom**
- Show that the flowers belong to Mom by writing the phrase correctly in the possessive noun column.
- Partner share a sentence using "Mom's flowers." (If time permits, choose a few students to share their sentences.)

Tim has a pet cat.
Tim **'s** cat is brown.

| Noun | Possessive Noun |
|------|-----------------|
| Tim  | Tim's cat       |

The cat **'s** toys are in the red bin.

**Answer Key**

| Noun | Possessive Noun |
|------|-----------------|
| Tim  | Tim's cat       |
| cat  | cat's toys      |
| Mom  | Mom's flowers   |

## Passage Reading

### UNDERLINE PATTERN WORDS

**Passage – Literary: *The Next Plan***

Now we'll practice finding closed syllable words with the c-h, s-h, t-h, or w-h consonant digraph patterns. Our passage today is about a kid who fell while she was running and hurt herself. She plans something fun for her friends while she rests.

Today we are going to look for closed syllable words with a consonant digraph and underline them.

The title does not have any words with a consonant digraph. Let's see if there are any on line 1. The word *path* has the final t-h consonant digraph pattern, so I make the closed syllable gesture and underline it. Help me find more words to underline. Hold up the closed syllable gesture when you see another word with a consonant digraph, and I'll underline it. (Continue underlining words with a consonant digraph to the black line.)

**Now it's your turn. Turn to page 19 in your Student Workbook. Here are the steps:**

1. **Begin at black line and continue to the end of the passage.**
2. **Use your fingers to find the vowel.**
3. **If you find a word with a c-h, s-h, t-h, or w-h consonant digraph, underline it.**
4. **Finally, whisper read the words you underlined.**

(Refer to the note under the passage on page 52 for exceptions.)

**I'll give you a few minutes and we'll check them together.**

## DAY 12

### Phonological Awareness Warm-Up

Today we are going to practice <u>deleting, or taking away, a sound at the beginning or end</u> of a word to make a new word.

**Watch me. My turn.**
- **The word is <u>cup</u>. I will delete /k/ from the beginning of the word. The new word is <u>up</u>.**

**Now, I will delete a sound from the end of a word. Watch me. My turn.**
- **The word is <u>wait</u>. I delete /t/ from the end of the word. The new word is <u>way</u>.**

**Let's practice a couple together.**
- **Say send: (send) Delete /s/ from the beginning. Word? end**
- **Say soap: (soap) Delete /p/ from the end. Word? so**

**Now it's your turn. Here are the directions:**
- **I'll say a word and you repeat it.**
- **Next, I'll tell you what sound to delete, or take away, from the beginning or end of the word.**
- **Then, tell me the new word. Ready?**

| | | | | |
|---|---|---|---|---|
| Say hair: (hair) Delete /h/ from the beginning. Word? | air | Say belt: (belt) Delete /t/ from the end. Word? | bell |
| Say farm: (farm) Delete /f/ from the beginning. Word? | arm | Say rake: (rake) Delete /k/ from the end. Word? | ray |
| Say clock: (clock) Delete /k/ from the beginning. Word? | lock | Say start: (start) Delete /t/ from the end. Word? | star |
| Say tray: (tray) Delete /t/ from the beginning. Word? | ray | Say made: (made) Delete /d/ from the end. Word? | may |
| Say meat: (meat) Delete /m/ from the beginning. Word? | eat | Say cart: (cart) Delete /t/ from the end. Word? | car |
| Say fear: (fear) Delete /f/ from the beginning. Word? | ear | Say heat: (heat) Delete /t/ from the end. Word? | he |
| Say slip: (slip) Delete /s/ from the beginning. Word? | lip | Say bite: (bite) Delete /t/ from the end. Word? | by |
| Say heart: (heart) Delete /h/ from the beginning. Word? | art | Say treat: (treat) Delete /t/ from the end. Word? | tree |

## Phonics Pattern

### READING PATTERN WORDS

#### Review the Pattern

We're continuing to read and spell words with the c-h, s-h, t-h, or w-h consonant digraph patterns.

**Repeat after me:** A consonant digraph has 1 sound spelled with 2 consonants side by side.

- **How do you pronounce the consonant digraph *c-h*?** /ch/
- **How do you pronounce the consonant digraph *s-h*?** /sh/
- **How do you pronounce the consonant digraph *t-h*?** /th/
- **How do you pronounce the consonant digraph *w-h*?** /hw/

**Now, let's review the closed syllable pattern. Say it with me:** Closed syllable words have 1 vowel letter followed by 1 or more consonants, and the vowel sound is short.

**Show me the gesture and say the syllable type.**  closed

#### Read Pattern Words

Now, we're going to read words with a c-h, s-h, t-h, or w-h consonant digraph.

When I show you a word, follow these steps:

1. Find the vowel or vowels and say the number of vowel letters.
2. If the vowel is followed by 1 or more consonants, say "yes." Say "no" if it is not.
3. Say the syllable type and show the gesture.
4. Say the vowel sound.
5. Say "initial" or "final" and the digraph, if there is one.
6. Read the word.

#### Answer Key

| Words on Presentation | |
|---|---|
| 1. (1, yes, closed, /ĕ/, initial c-h) - chest | 6. (1, yes, closed, /ĭ/, no) - fill |
| 2. (1, yes, closed, /ă/, no) - mat | 7. (1, yes, closed, /ĕ/, initial s-h) - shed |
| 3. (1, yes, closed, /ĭ/, no) - list | 8. (1, yes, closed, /ĕ/, final s-h) - fresh |
| 4. (1, yes, closed, /ă/, final t-h) - math | 9. (1, yes, closed, /ĭ/, no) - him |
| 5. (1, yes, closed, /ĭ/, initial w-h) - whim | 10. (1, yes, closed, /ĭ/, final c-h) - rich |

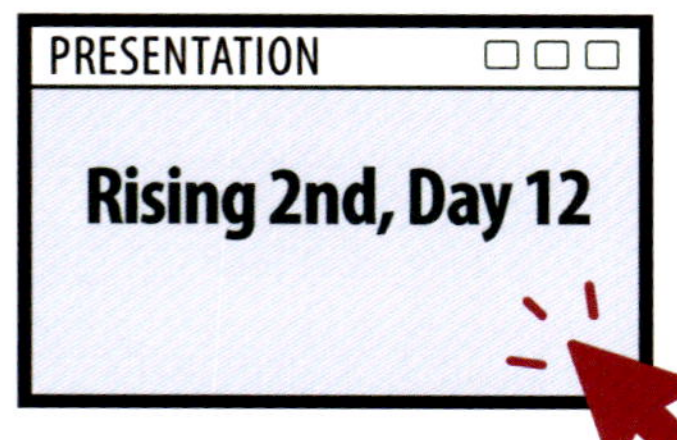


**Note:** Display the Sound-Spelling Cards for the consonant digraphs so the students have a visual cue to reference throughout the lesson.

**Routine for Word Reading:**

- Find the vowels.
- How many vowel letters?
- Is it followed by 1 or more consonants?
- Syllable type and gesture?
- Vowel sound?
- Is there a consonant digraph? Which one?
- Word?

| | |
|---|---|
| 1. chest | 6. fill |
| 2. mat | 7. shed |
| 3. list | 8. fresh |
| 4. math | 9. him |
| 5. whim | 10. rich |

## Phonics Pattern

### SORT WORDS

Let's practice identifying words that fit the pattern and words that
do not.

**Watch what I do.**

(Display shelf.)

**The first word is shelf.**

- **First, I find the vowel and identify the syllable type.**
- **I see 1 vowel letter followed by 1 or more consonants.**
- **This word follows the closed syllable pattern.**
- **I whisper "closed" while making the closed gesture.**
- **Then, I whisper the vowel sound /ĕ/.**
- **Now, I check for the c-h, s-h, t-h, or w-h consonant digraphs before
  or after the vowel. There is the consonant digraph *s-h* before
  the vowel.**
- **I place the word *shelf* in the initial /sh/ shoe column.**
- **Finally, I slide my finger under the word and
  whisper "shelf."**

| chair | branch | shoe | brush |
|-------|--------|------|-------|
|       |        | shelf |      |

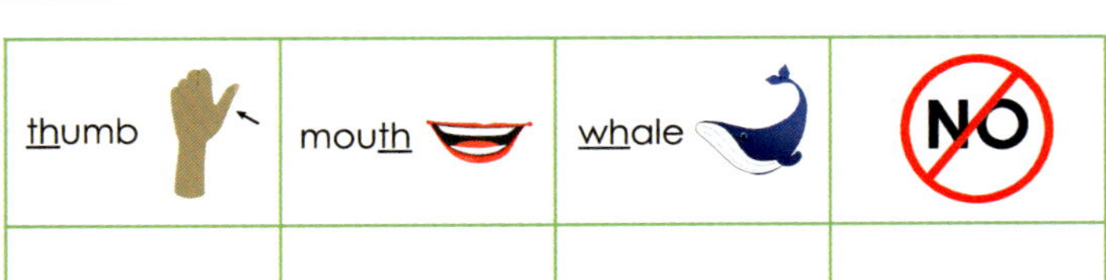

| thumb | mouth | whale | NO |
|-------|-------|-------|-----|
|       |       |       |     |

**Now it's your turn. Turn to page 20 in your Student Workbook.
Let's review the steps.**

1. **Look at the word to decide if it follows the closed syllable pattern.**
2. **Whisper the syllable type and gesture.**
3. **Whisper the vowel sound.**
4. **Look for a c-h, s-h, t-h, or w-h consonant digraph.**
5. **Write the word in the correct column.**
6. **Finally, whisper read all the words in each column.**

**I'll check back with you in a few minutes and then you can
check your answers.**

### Routine for Word Sorting:

- **Find the vowel or vowels.**
- **How many vowel letters?**
- **Is there 1 or more
  consonants after the vowel?**
- **Syllable type gesture?**
- **Vowel sound?**
- **Is there a consonant digraph
  *c-h, s-h, t-h,* or *w-h*?**
- **Initial or final?**
- **Where does this word go?**
- **Read the words.**

## Answer Key

| | | | |
|---|---|---|---|
| <u>ch</u>air | bran<u>ch</u> | <u>sh</u>oe | bru<u>sh</u> |
| chest | pinch | shelf | fish |
| | such | | |

| | | | |
|---|---|---|---|
| <u>th</u>umb | mou<u>th</u> | <u>wh</u>ale | NO |
| thin | tenth | when | crest |
| with | | fist | |

| | |
|---|---|
| 1. tenth | 6. crest |
| 2. chest | 7. when |
| 3. fish | 8. with |
| 4. pinch | 9. such |
| 5. thin | 10. fist |

## Writing

### SOUND-SPELLING MAPPING

Now we're going to spell words that have the c-h, s-h, t-h, or w-h consonant digraph patterns. We've done sound-spelling mapping before. Let's do one together.

The word is <u>shop</u>. Word? **shop**
- Finger-stretch and say the sounds. **/sh/ /ŏ/ /p/**
- How many sounds? **3** How many boxes? **3**
- We need 3 boxes. We tap and place a dot in the bottom right corner for each sound. **/sh/ /ŏ/ /p/**
- Now, we write the letters.
  - Which letter or letters spell the /sh/ sound? **s-h** Which box? **first**
  - Which letter spells the /ŏ/ sound? **o** Which box? **second**
  - Which letter spells the /p/ sound? **p** Which box? **third**
- Syllable type and gesture? **closed**
- Sounds? **/sh/ /ŏ/ /p/**
- Word? **shop**

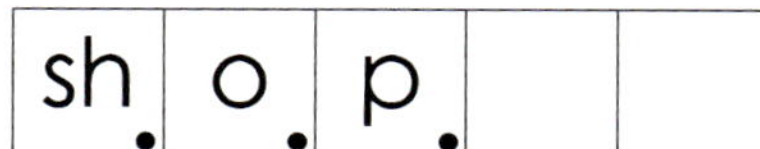

 Now it's your turn. Turn to page 20 in your Student Workbook. Here are the steps:

1. Finger-stretch while saying the sounds.
2. Count the sounds.
3. Place a dot in the bottom right corner of the boxes you'll need.
4. Write the letters. Remember that each sound gets its own box.
5. Look for an initial or final c-h, s-h, t-h, or w-h consonant digraph.
6. Whisper the syllable type and read the word to yourself.

## Answer Key

| Words to Dictate | Correct Answers in Student Workbook |
|---|---|
| shop | sh o p |
| 1. chip | ch i p |
| 2. quick | qu i ck |
| 3. dash | d a sh |
| 4. then | th e n |
| 5. split | s p l i t |
| 6. munch | m u n ch |

***Note:*** In the word *quick* (#2), the letters *q* and *u* are mapped in the box close to the line that separates them. These letters are mapped in this format to show that, although each letter makes a separate sound, the letter *u* always follows the q when it appears in a word. This shows that the 2 letters work together.

## Passage Reading

### READ PASSAGE

#### Passage – Literary: *The Next Plan*

Now we'll read the passage we underlined yesterday. Let's read to find out what fun plan the kid has for her friends while she recovers from a running accident.

First, we'll read some of the underlined words together. When you see a consonant digraph in the underlined words, make the closed syllable gesture and read the word. What is the first underlined word? path Read with me just the underlined words above the black line.

Now it's your turn. Turn to page 19 in your Student Workbook. Here are the steps:

1. First, whisper read all the underlined words in the rest of the passage.
2. Then, go back to the beginning and whisper read the passage.

## Comprehension

### WRITTEN RESPONSE

Turn to page 21 in your Student Workbook. Use the graphic organizer to make short notes about 1 detail that happened in the beginning, middle, and end of this passage. I'll give you 5 minutes and then ask a few of you to share. (RL.1.2)

## Answer Key (answers vary)

| Beginning | Middle | End |
|---|---|---|
| The kid liked to go to the rock path to run and get fit. She fell and got hurt. | The kid planned a magic show as she got better. | The kid had a magic show for friends. It was a smash hit. |

# DAY 13

## Phonological Awareness Warm-Up

Today we are going to practice <u>substituting, or changing, a sound</u> at <u>the beginning</u> of a word to make a new word.

**Watch me. My turn.**
- The word is <u>ship</u>. I change /sh/ to /ch/ at the beginning of the word. The new word is <u>chip</u>.

**Let's practice one together.**
- Say nice: (**nice**) Change /n/ to /m/. Word? **mice**

**Now it's your turn. Here are the directions:**
- I'll say a word and you repeat it.
- Next, I'll tell you what sound to substitute, or change, at the beginning of the word.
- Then, tell me the new word. Ready?

| | | | | |
|---|---|---|---|---|
| Say bad: (**bad**) Change /b/ to /m/. Word? | **mad** | Say car: (**car**) Change /k/ to /f/. Word? | **far** |
| Say rest: (**rest**) Change /r/ to /b/. Word? | **best** | Say sea: (**sea**) Change /s/ to /m/. Word? | **me** |
| Say book: (**book**) Change /b/ to /l/. Word? | **look** | Say race: (**race**) Change /r/ to /f/. Word? | **face** |
| Say shoot: (**shoot**) Change /sh/ to /b/. Word? | **boot** | Say sock: (**sock**) Change /s/ to /l/. Word? | **lock** |
| Say cry: (**cry**) Change /k/ to /f/. Word? | **fry** | Say phone: (**phone**) Change /f/ to /b/. Word? | **bone** |
| Say hut: (**hut**) Change /h/ to /k/. Word? | **cut** | Say head: (**head**) Change /h/ to /b/. Word? | **bed** |
| Say map: (**map**) Change /m/ to /r/. Word? | **rap** | Say rag: (**rag**) Change /r/ to /b/. Word? | **bag** |
| Say chair: (**chair**) Change /ch/ to /f/. Word? | **fair** | Say shack: (**shack**) Change /sh/ to /b/. Word? | **back** |

## Phonics Pattern

### WORD READING ACCURACY

Look at the words. Let's read them together. As you read each word, hold up the closed syllable gesture. For the last 2 words, show the closed gesture with both hands for each of the 2 syllables while reading the words.

| | | | |
|---|---|---|---|
| cash | wish | shop | bunch |
| thank | when | dash | think |
| math | chat | rich | which |
| that | chip | bath | dish |
| ship | tenth | sudden | chipmunk |

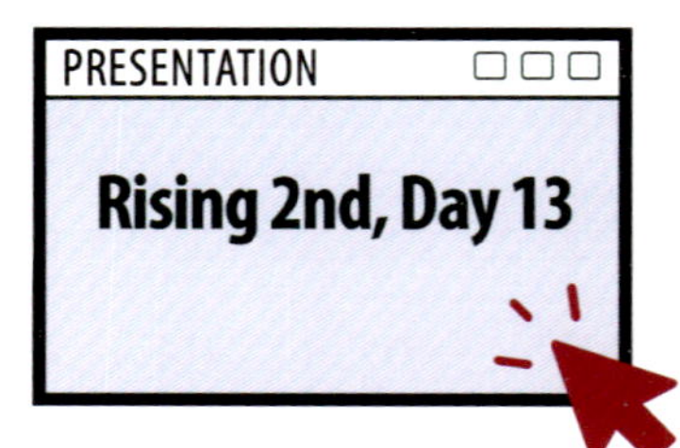

## Writing

### SENTENCE WRITING

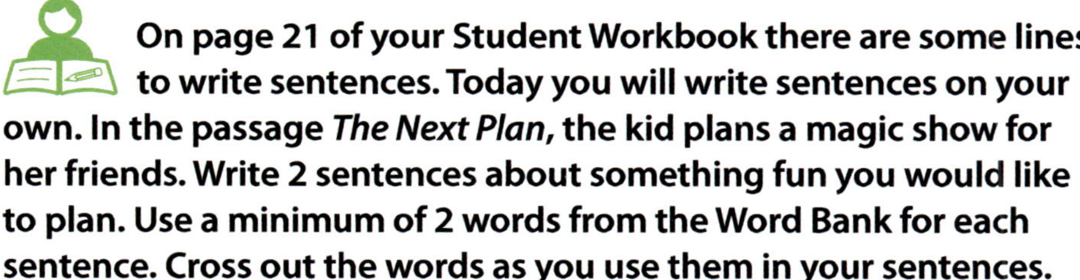 On page 21 of your Student Workbook there are some lines to write sentences. Today you will write sentences on your own. In the passage *The Next Plan*, the kid plans a magic show for her friends. Write 2 sentences about something fun you would like to plan. Use a minimum of 2 words from the Word Bank for each sentence. Cross out the words as you use them in your sentences.

| Word Bank | | | | |
|---|---|---|---|---|
| chip | wish | shop | cash | know |
| tenth | which | that | when | thick |
| of | after | could | him | her |

## Writing

### SOUND-SPELLING MAPPING

Now we're going to spell words that have the c-h, s-h, t-h, or w-h consonant digraph patterns. We've done sound-spelling mapping before. Let's do one together.

**The word is <u>which</u>. Word? which**

- **Finger-stretch and say the sounds. /hw/ /ĭ/ /ch/**
- **How many sounds? 3 How many boxes? 3**
- **We need 3 boxes. We tap and place a dot in the bottom right corner for each sound. /hw/ /ĭ/ /ch/**
- **Now, we write the letters.**
  - **Which letter or letters spell the /hw/ sound? w-h Which box? first**
  - **Which letter spells the /ĭ/ sound? i Which box? second**
  - **Which letter or letters spell the /ch/ sound? c-h Which box? third**
- **How many consonant digraphs are in this word? 2**
  - **Yes, this word has an initial w-h and a final c-h.**
- **Syllable type and gesture? closed**
- **Sounds? /hw/ /ĭ/ /ch/**
- **Word? which**

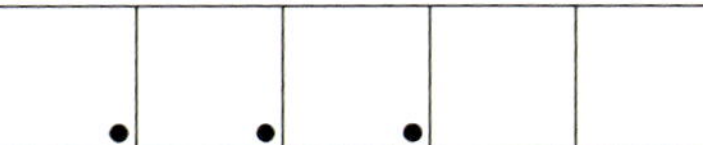
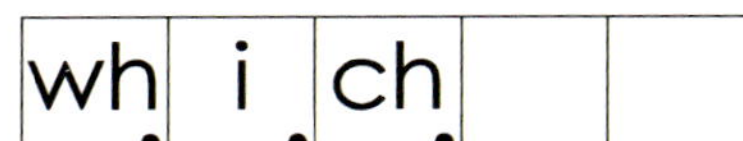

**Day 13**

Now it's your turn. Turn to page 22 in your Student Workbook. Here are the steps:

1. Finger-stretch while saying the sounds.
2. Count the sounds.
3. Place a dot in the bottom right corner of the boxes you'll need.
4. Write the letters. Remember that each sound gets its own box.
5. Look for an initial or final c-h, s-h, t-h, or w-h consonant digraph.
6. Whisper the syllable type and read the word to yourself.

**Answer Key**

| Words to Dictate | Correct Answers in Student Workbook |
|---|---|
| which | wh i ch |
| 1. stand | s t a n d |
| 2. champ | ch a m p |
| 3. ranch | r a n ch |
| 4. blast | b l a s t |
| 5. crash | c r a sh |

## Writing

### CONTRACTIONS

Today we will review contractions. Contractions occur when 2 words are put together and shortened into 1 word. Read these contractions with me:

(Display contractions.)
- **I'm**
- **don't**

I'm
don't

**Which two words make up the contraction *I'm*?** I am
**Which letter is replaced with an apostrophe?** a

(Display sentence.)
**Read this sentence with me.** I'm her little sis.

I'm her little sis.

**Which two words make up the contraction *don't*?** do not
**Which letter is replaced with an apostrophe?** the second o

(Display sentence.)
**Read this sentence with me.** I don't want to go to the shop.

I don't want to go to the shop.

(Display it's.)
**Let's review 1 more contraction.**

**The contraction is it's.**
- **Which word do you recognize in this contraction?** it
- *It's* **means the same thing as** *it is*. **This is just a shortened way to use those words in our writing and speaking.**
- **In the contraction** *it's*, **which letter or letters are replaced with an apostrophe?** i
  - **Yes, the second vowel** *i* **is dropped.**
- **Spell the contraction** *it's* **with me. Don't forget to say "apostrophe."** i-t-apostrophe-s
- **Word?** it's
- **Partner share a sentence using the contraction** *it's*.

it is

| 2 Words | Combine Words and Slash | Contraction |
|---------|--------------------------|-------------|
| it is | it i̷s | it's |

**Now it's your turn. Turn to page 22 in your Student Workbook. Here are the steps:**

1. **Look at the 2 words in the first column.**
2. **Combine them in the middle column.**
3. **Draw a slash through the letter to be removed.**
4. **Then, write the contraction in the last column; don't forget the apostrophe.**
5. **Whisper read the contraction to yourself.**

### Answer Key

| 2 Words | Combine Words and Slash | Contraction |
|---------|--------------------------|-------------|
| it is | it i̷s | it's |
| I am | I a̷m | I'm |
| do not | do no̷t | don't |

*Note:* As an extension for application, have students use the blank space under the table in their workbooks to write a sentence using each of the contractions.

Day
**13**

## Passage Reading

### UNDERLINE/CIRCLE PATTERN WORDS

### Passage – Informational: *Chipmunks*

Now it's time to practice with a new passage. This passage is about chipmunks. Chipmunks are small mammals that like to run and hide in bushes, shrubs, and grass. A mammal is an animal that has hair or fur, breathes air, and has a backbone.

We'll underline only the closed syllable words with c-h, s-h, t-h, or w-h consonant digraph patterns like we've done before. We will also circle any 2-syllable words that have 2 closed syllables. Let's begin with the title. Which is the first word to underline or circle? chipmunks Do we underline or circle it? circle Why? It is a 2-syllable word. I make the closed syllable gesture with 2 hands under both syllables *chip* and *munks* and then circle it. (Draw a line between the p and m in chipmunks to model the syllable division.)

Help me find more closed syllable words with the c-h, s-h, t-h, or w-h consonant digraph patterns and multisyllable words. If you see a consonant digraph, use 1 hand to make a closed syllable gesture and I will underline the word. If you see a 2-syllable word, use 2 hands to make 2 closed syllable gestures and I will circle the word. (Continue underlining and circling to the black line.)

Now it's your turn. Turn to page 23 in your Student Workbook. Here are the steps:

1. Begin at black line and continue to the end of the passage.
2. Use your fingers to find the vowel or vowels.
3. If you find a word with a c-h, s-h, t-h, or w-h consonant digraph, underline it. If you find a multisyllable word with 2 closed syllables, circle it.
4. Finally, whisper read the words you underlined or circled.

(Refer to the note under the passage on page 53 for exceptions.)

I'll give you a few minutes and then we'll check them together.

# DAY 14

## Phonological Awareness Warm-Up

Today we are going to practice <u>substituting</u>, or changing, a sound at <u>the end</u> of a word to make a new word.

**Watch me. My turn.**
- **The word is <u>push</u>. I change /sh/ to /t/ at the end of the word. The new word is <u>put</u>.**

**Let's practice one together.**
- **Say seat: (seat) Change /t/ to /d/. Word? seed**

**Now it's your turn. Here are the directions:**
- **I'll say a word and you repeat it.**
- **Next, I'll tell you what sound to change at the end of the word.**
- **Then, tell me the new word. Ready?**

| | | | | | |
|---|---|---|---|---|---|
| Say mark: (mark) Change /k/ to /t/. Word? | **mart** | Say rat: (rat) Change /t/ to /sh/. Word? | **rash** |
| Say beat: (beat) Change /t/ to /ch/. Word? | **beach** | Say trash: (trash) Change /sh/ to /k/. Word? | **track** |
| Say great: (great) Change /t/ to /p/. Word? | **grape** | Say shape: (shape) Change /p/ to /k/. Word? | **shake** |
| Say take: (take) Change /k/ to /p/. Word? | **tape** | Say cash: (cash) Change /sh/ to /t/. Word? | **cat** |
| Say trip: (trip) Change /p/ to /k/. Word? | **trick** | Say card: (card) Change /d/ to /t/. Word? | **cart** |
| Say shop: (shop) Change /p/ to /t/. Word? | **shot** | Say back: (back) Change /k/ to /t/. Word? | **bat** |
| Say ride: (ride) Change /d/ to /z/. Word? | **rise** | Say mat: (mat) Change /t/ to /sh/. Word? | **mash** |
| Say bite: (bite) Change /t/ to /k/. Word? | **bike** | Say part: (part) Change /t/ to /k/. Word? | **park** |

## Phonics Pattern

### SORT SYLLABLES

Let's practice identifying, sorting, and reading the syllables in multisyllable words. Watch me model with the first word.

(Display <u>himself</u>.)
**Here is the word.** (Do not read the word.)

**Step 1: Find the vowels.**
- **I use both hands to find the vowels in each syllable.**
- **I point to the letter *i* with my left pointer finger and the letter *e* with my right pointer finger.**
- **There are 2 vowel sounds.**

**Step 2: Underline the vowels.**
- **Next, I underline the vowels.**
- **This word has 2 syllables because it has 2 vowel sounds.**

**Step 3: Draw a line between the syllables.**
- I look for the number of consonants between the vowels.
- There are 2 — m and s. When there are 2 consonants between the 2 vowels, divide the word between them.
- I draw a syllable division line between the letters *m* and *s*.

him|self

**Step 4: Sort each syllable.**

| Sort the first syllable. | Sort the second syllable. |
|---|---|
| I cover the second syllable and look at the first one.<br>• The syllable type and gesture are closed.<br>• The vowel sound is /ĭ/.<br>• The syllable is him.<br>I write the syllable *him* under First Syllable. | I cover the first syllable and look at the second one.<br>• The syllable type and gesture are closed.<br>• The vowel sound is /ĕ/.<br>• The syllable is self.<br>I write the syllable *self* under Second Syllable. |

**Step 5: Read the word.**
- The word is himself.

| Word | First Syllable | Second Syllable |
|---|---|---|
| him|self | him | self |

**Let's try one together. I'll answer and gesture with you.**
(Students should be pointing and gesturing throughout the routine.)

(Display chipmunk.)
**Here is the word.** (Do not read the word.)

**Step 1: Find the vowels.**
- Use both hands to find the vowels in each syllable.
- Point to the letter *i* with the left pointer finger and the letter *u* with the right pointer finger.
- How many vowel sounds? 2

chipmunk

**Step 2: Underline the vowels.**
- Next, we underline the vowels.
- This word has 2 vowel sounds. How many syllables are there? 2

chipmunk

**Step 3: Draw a line between the syllables.**
- How many consonants are between the vowel sounds? 2
- Where do I draw the line? between the *p* and *m*
- I draw a syllable division line between the letters *p* and *m*.

chip|munk

Day
**14**

**Step 4:** Sort each syllable.

| | |
|---|---|
| **Sort the first syllable.** <br> **Cover the second syllable and look at the first one.** <br> • **Syllable type?** closed <br> • **Vowel sound?** /ĭ/ <br> • **Syllable?** chip <br> I write the syllable *chip* under First Syllable. | **Sort the second syllable.** <br> **Cover the first syllable and look at the second one.** <br> • **Syllable type?** closed <br> • **Vowel sound?** /ŭ/ <br> • **Syllable?** munk <br> I write the syllable *munk* under Second Syllable. |

**Step 5:** Read the word.
- **Word?** chipmunk

| Word | First Syllable | Second Syllable |
|---|---|---|
| chip\|munk | chip | munk |

**Now it's your turn. Turn to page 24 in your Student Workbook. Here are the steps:**

1. **Find the vowels and underline them.**
2. **Count the consonants between the vowels. Remember, when there are 2 consonants, divide between them.**
3. **Draw a line between the syllables.**
4. **Sort each syllable.**
   - **Say the syllable type and show the gesture.**
   - **Say the vowel sound and read the syllable.**
   - **Write the syllable in the correct column.**
5. **Read the word.**

**Answer Key**

| Word | First Syllable | Second Syllable |
|---|---|---|
| chip\|munk | chip | munk |
| 1. mag\|net | mag | net |
| 2. sud\|den | sud | den |
| 3. rab\|bit | rab | bit |
| 4. traf\|fic | traf | fic |
| 5. in\|sect | in | sect |

**Routine for Sorting Syllables:**

- Underline the vowels.
- How many consonants between the vowels?
- Draw a line to divide syllables.
- Sort each syllable.
  - Syllable type and gesture?
  - Vowel sound?
  - Read the syllable.
- Word?

**Day 14**

## Writing

### INFLECTED ENDINGS

**Now we'll learn how to add the endings *-er* and *-est* to an adjective. An adjective is a describing word. Let's look at this table, which explains the rules for adding -er and -est to words.**

| Rule | Adjective | New Word | Spelling Rules |
|------|-----------|----------|----------------|
| 1 | hard | harder, hardest | For words spelled with <u>2 or more consonants at the end</u>, add -er or -est. |
| 2 | pretty | prettier, prettiest | For words spelled with <u>y at the end</u>, <u>drop the last y and add i</u> before adding -er or -est. |
| 3 | hot | hotter, hottest | For words spelled with <u>a single vowel followed by 1 consonant, double the final consonant</u> before adding -er or -est. |

**Watch what I do.**

(Display <u>big</u>.)

**The word is <u>big</u>.**

- **I find the vowel and touch under it.**
- **The word *big* has 1 vowel letter *i* followed by 1 consonant *g*. This follows rule 3, so I double the consonant *g* before adding the -er or -est.**

- **I write the word *bigger* under "Word + er" and *biggest* under "Word + est".**
- **I read each word: big, bigger, and biggest.**

| Word | Word + er | Word + est |
|------|-----------|------------|
| big – rule 3 | bigger | biggest |

 **Now it's your turn. Turn to page 24 in your Student Workbook. Here are the steps:**

1. **Read the word.**
2. **Check for the number of consonants or the letter *y* after the vowel.**
3. **Then, decide which rule to use and write the rule number next to the word in the first column.**
4. **Write the word plus the -er and the -est using the correct spelling rule.**
5. **Finally, read the words.**

## Answer Key

| Word | Word + er | Word + est |
|---|---|---|
| big – rule 3 | bigger | biggest |
| 1.  funny – rule 2 | funnier | funniest |
| 2.  rich – rule 1 | richer | richest |
| 3.  wet – rule 3 | wetter | wettest |

## Writing

### WORD CHAINS

It's word chain time! We've done this on other days. Remember how we begin with 1 word and then spell others in a chain? We'll add, delete, or change 1 sound at a time to spell a new word.

Let's do this first one together.

**The first word is ship.**
**Let's change ship to chip.**
- **Which sound changes?** /sh/ changes to /ch/
- **Which letter changes?** change the letter *s* to *c*

I write the word *chip* under *ship*.

**Next, I change chip to chop.**
- **Which sound changes?** /ĭ/ changes to /ŏ/
- **Which letter changes?** change the letter *i* to *o*

I write the word *chop* under *chip*.

**Finally, I change chop to shop.**
- **Which sound changes?** /ch/ changes to /sh/
- **Which letter changes?** change the letter *c* to *s*

I write the word *shop* under *chop*.

| |
|---|
| ship |
| chip |
| chop |
| shop |

**Now it's your turn. Turn to page 25 in your Student Workbook. You'll find a spot to write 3 word chains. I'll tell you 1 word at a time and you'll write each new word below the old one. Find the page and look up when you're ready.**

*Note:* If you are writing the words on the board, make sure you build the words going down, not across.

**Routine for Word Chains:**
- Change word *x* to word *y*.
  - Which sound changes?
  - Which letter(s) changes?
- Write word *y* under word *x*.

## Answer Key

| |
|---|
| wish |
| with |
| will |
| chill |

| |
|---|
| cash |
| crash |
| trash |
| track |

| |
|---|
| whim |
| dim |
| dish |
| dash |

*Note:* Tell students that the /hw/ sound in the word *whim*, in the final word chain, is spelled with a consonant digraph.

## Passage Reading

### READ PASSAGE

### Passage – Informational: *Chipmunks*

**Now it's time to read a new passage. This passage is all about chipmunks. What do you already know about chipmunks?**

 **Turn to page 23. First, we will read the passage aloud together. While we're reading, think about the main topic of the passage.**

(Guide class in chorally reading the passage, starting with the title.)

## Comprehension

### WRITTEN RESPONSE

**Now turn to page 25 in your student workbook. Let's complete a graphic organizer about the main topic and key details for the passage we just read.  (RI.1.2)** (Display graphic organizer.)

- **What is the title of the passage we just read? Chipmunks Write this in your graphic organizer. Don't forget to capitalize the title.**

- **What is the main topic of this passage? small animals called chipmunks**
  - **Write the sentence "There are small animals called chipmunks." in the Main Topic section of your graphic organizer.**

| **Title:** Chipmunks |
| --- |
| **Main Topic** |
| There are small animals called chipmunks. |
| **Key Details** |
| 1. |
| 2. |
| 3. |

- **What are some key details that we learned about chipmunks?** (List students' responses on a whiteboard or flipchart. Answers may include: little mammals, brown, live in nests, run and jump, like nuts, have hands, not good pets, etc.)

- **Select 3 key details that are most interesting to you. Write them in complete sentences in your graphic organizer.**

# DAY 15

## Phonological Awareness Warm-Up

Today we are going to practice <u>substituting, or changing, a sound in the middle</u> of a word to make a new word.

**Watch me. My turn.**
- The word is <u>flat</u>. I change /ă/ to /ō/ in the middle of the word. The new word is <u>float</u>.

**Let's practice one together.**
- Say ham: (**ham**) Change /ă/ to /ŭ/. Word? **hum**

**Now it's your turn. Here are the directions:**
- I'll say a word and you repeat it.
- Next, I'll tell you what sound to change in the middle of the word.
- Then, tell me the new word. Ready?

| | | | |
|---|---|---|---|
| Say side: (**side**) Change /ī/ to /ă/. Word? | **sad** | Say hit: (**hit**) Change /ĭ/ to /ă/. Word? | **hat** |
| Say team: (**team**) Change /ē/ to /ī/. Word? | **time** | Say lock: (**lock**) Change /ŏ/ to /ĭ/. Word? | **lick** |
| Say pack: (**pack**) Change /ă/ to /ĭ/. Word? | **pick** | Say bat: (**bat**) Change /ă/ to /ō/. Word? | **boat** |
| Say check: (**check**) Change /ĕ/ to /ĭ/. Word? | **chick** | Say bag: (**bag**) Change /ă/ to /ĭ/. Word? | **big** |
| Say tried: (**tried**) Change /ī/ to /ā/. Word? | **trade** | Say flight: (**flight**) Change /ī/ to /ă/. Word? | **flat** |
| Say shop: (**shop**) Change /ŏ/ to /ā/. Word? | **shape** | Say can: (**can**) Change /ă/ to /ā/. Word? | **cane** |
| Say cap: (**cap**) Change /ă/ to /ō/. Word? | **cope** | Say luck: (**luck**) Change /ŭ/ to /ī/. Word? | **like** |
| Say rap: (**rap**) Change /ă/ to /ō/. Word? | **rope** | Say mean: (**mean**) Change /ē/ to /ă/. Word? | **man** |

## Writing

### SYLLABLE MAPPING

Today we're going to practice spelling 2-syllable words with the closed syllable pattern. Watch how I use the Syllable Mapping paper. Each box holds 1 syllable.

**The word is <u>bathtub</u>.**
- **I tap one box for each syllable I hear: bath/tub.** (Place your hand under your chin while saying the syllables. Point out that your chin drops as you say each syllable.)
- **There are 2 syllables.**
- **Now, I write the letters that spell the sounds in each syllable.**
  - I write the first syllable, *bath*, in the first box: /b/ letter *b*, /ă/ letter *a*, /th/ letters *t-h*.
  - I write the second syllable, *tub*, in the second box: /t/ letter *t*, /ŭ/ letter *u*, /b/ letter *b*.

PRESENTATION ☐ ☐ ☐

**Rising 2nd, Day 15**

| | |
|---|---|
| | |
| bath | |
| bath | tub |

- **The syllables are closed-closed.** (Gesture using both hands under each syllable.)
- **I slide a finger under each syllable, combining them, and whisper "bathtub."**

**Let's do one together.**

**The word is <u>contest</u>. Word?** contest

- **I tap each box while we say the syllables.** con/test **How many syllables?** 2
- **Now, I write the letters that spell the sounds in each syllable.**
- **First syllable?** con
  - **Sounds?** /k/ /ŏ/ /n/
  - **Letters?** c-o-n in the first box
- **Second syllable?** test
  - **Sounds?** /t/ /ĕ/ /s/ /t/
  - **Letters?** t-e-s-t in the second box
- **Syllables?** closed-closed (Use 2 hands to gesture for 2 closed syllables.)
- **Word?** contest

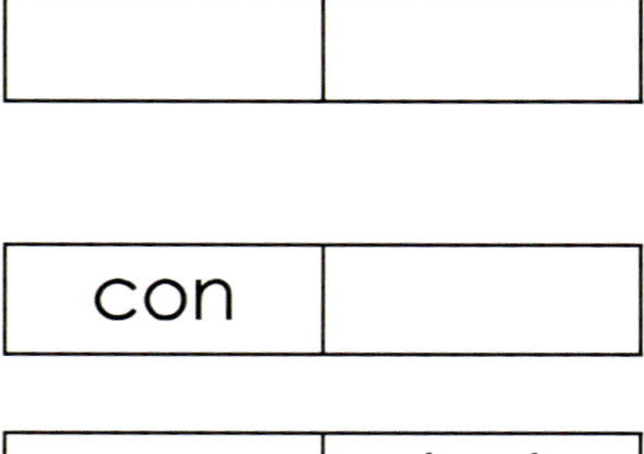

**Now it's your turn. Turn to page 26 in your Student Workbook. Here are the steps:**

1. **Say the word.**
2. **Tap a box for each syllable you hear.**
3. **For each syllable, say the sounds, write the letters, and say the syllable type while showing the gesture.**
4. **Slide your finger under both syllables and whisper read the word to yourself.**

*Note:* Remind students that they can finger-stretch sounds to spell the syllables.

**Answer Key**

| Words to Dictate | Correct Answers in Student Workbook | |
| --- | --- | --- |
| contest | con | test |
| 1. velvet | vel | vet |
| 2. chipmunk | chip | munk |
| 3. dentist | den | tist |
| 4. rumpus | rum | pus |
| 5. witness | wit | ness |

*Note:* When dictating the words, give a brief definition of each word. The meanings will be helpful in comprehension of the passages. For example, the word *rumpus* means a "noisy disturbance."

## Writing

### CONTRACTIONS

Today we'll review more contractions. Remember, contractions occur when 2 words are put together and shortened into 1 word. An apostrophe is used to show where a letter or letters are dropped. Read these contractions with me:

(Display contractions.)

- **let's**
- **I'll**
- **didn't**

**Which 2 words make up the contraction** *let's*? **let us**
**Which letter is replaced with an apostrophe? u**

(Display sentence.)
**Read this sentence with me. Let's fish in the pond.**



**Which 2 words make up the contraction** *I'll*? **I will**
**Which letter or letters are replaced with an apostrophe? w-i**

(Display sentence.)
**Read this sentence with me. I'll pack my lunch.**



**Which 2 words make up the contraction** *didn't*? **did not**
**Which letter is replaced with an apostrophe? o**

(Display sentence.)
**Read this sentence with me. Rich didn't play in the mud.**



**Let's try another contraction.**

(Display I'm.)
**The contraction is I'm.**

- **Which word do you recognize in this contraction? I**
- *I'm* **means the same thing as** *I am*; **it is just a shortened way to use those words in our writing and speaking.**
- **In the contraction** *I'm*, **which letter or letters are replaced with an apostrophe? a**
  - Yes, the letter *a* is dropped.
- **Spell the contraction** *I'm* **with me. Don't forget to say "apostrophe." I-apostrophe-m**
- **Word? I'm**
- **Partner share a sentence using the contraction** *I'm*.

| 2 Words | Combine Words and Slash | Contraction |
| --- | --- | --- |
| I am | I a̸m | I'm |

 **Now it's your turn. Turn to page 26 in your Student Workbook. Here are the steps:**

1. Look at the words in the first column.
2. Combine them in the middle column.
3. Draw a slash through the letter or letters to be removed.
4. Then, write the contraction in the last column; don't forget the apostrophe.
5. Whisper read the contraction to yourself.
6. Finally, write 1 sentence using 1 of the contractions.

**Answer Key**

| 2 Words | Combine Words and Slash | Contraction |
|---|---|---|
| I am | I a̸m | I'm |
| do not | do n̸o̸t | don't |
| it is | it i̸s | it's |
| cannot | can n̸o̸t | can't |

(Check for complete sentences and the use of at least one contraction.)

 ## Fluency

### WORDS

We've been learning to read closed syllable words with consonant digraphs.

Look at this word grid. Please read it aloud chorally as a class. Ready?

| dash | them | which | with |
|---|---|---|---|
| chest | branch | that | when |

**Now it's your turn. Turn to page 27 in your Student Workbook. When I say "begin," point to the first word. Whisper read across the page. If you finish before I say "stop," start at the top and read the words again.** (Time students for 1 minute. Say "stop" and ask students to circle the last word that was read.)

| stash | branch | which | chest |
|---|---|---|---|
| that | shrub | this | dash |
| with | when | then | smash |
| chomp | them | path | whim |

## PHRASES

**We're going to read phrases. Let's practice 4 phrases together.**

| from the ranch | smash the dish | chit chat for fun | stash the trash |

**Now it's your turn. Turn to page 27 in your Student Workbook. When I say "begin," point to the first phrase and whisper it. Continue reading across the page. If you finish before I say "stop," start at the top and read the phrases again.** (Time students for 1 minute. Say "stop" and ask students to circle the last phrase that was read.)

| stash the trash | after we fish | to the old shed | chit chat for fun |
| chop the branch | in a rush | shut the bin | know a wish |
| to the ship | on the shelf | from the ranch | crack of the whip |
| smash the dish | see the chimp | could be a chip | just a flash |

## Passage Reading

### READ PASSAGES

**Today you are going to practice reading both of the passages. One was about a kid who entertained her friends as she rested from an injury. The other passage was about chipmunks.**

## Comprehension

### WRITTEN RESPONSE

**Turn to page 27 in your Student Workbook. Read both passages, and then write the answers to the question for each passage in your workbook.**

**Passage – Literary: *The Next Plan* on page 19**
  1. **Where did the kid like to run?  (RL.1.1)**  (up the hill on the rock path)

**Passage – Informational: *Chipmunks* on page 23**
  1. **How do chipmunks eat the nuts they like munching on?  (RI.1.1)** (They hold them in their hands, spit out the shells, and munch the pulp.)

# Jude's June Hike

1  Jude woke up to the sunrise just in time to take a hike to see her pal Pete.

2  In June, Jude is nine! She liked to take the time to think of life on the hike.

3  Jude hiked for quite some time. She had hiked five miles when she came

4  to Lone Lake Lane. Her pal Pete stays in a home on that side of the lake. For a

5  long time, Jude has missed her pal Pete.

6  Jude went in the front gate at his home and chimed the bell. Jude did not

7  see Pete but she did see a note on the side path. Pete left a note for Jude to

8  come inside. Jude did not like to be rude, but she felt safe with the note from

9  her pal.

10  When Jude went inside, she got quite the prize. All of her pals from class

11  were lined up on the sides. Jake, Mike, Eve, and the rest of her mates broke out

12  in smiles! Pete and his mom had baked homemade cupcakes. The pals ate the

13  cake and played games. It was a fine time to shine with a home full of Jude and

14  her best pals.

15  When it got late, Jude said she had one of the best times of her life.

16  Her prized pals made her smile.

**Note:** Although the words *come*, *one*, *some*, and *were* appear to follow the long vowel silent-e pattern, these words do not have a long vowel sound.

| Long Vowel Silent-e | | | | | | | | | Long Vowel Silent-e, Simple Multisyllable | Word Count* |
|---|---|---|---|---|---|---|---|---|---|---|
| **Long a** | | **Long e** | | **Long i** | | | **Long o** | **Long u** | | 223 |
| ate | Jake | safe | Eve | chime | line | shine | broke | Jude | cupcake | **Pattern Words** |
| bake | lake | take | Pete | fine | Mike | side | home | June | homemade | 84 (38%) |
| cake | lane | | | five | mile | smile | lone | rude | inside | * including title |
| came | late | | | hike | nine | time | note | | sunrise | |
| game | made | | | life | prize | | woke | | | |
| gate | mate | | | like | quite | | | | | |

   95 Phonics Booster Bundle™: Summer School Edition 2021 • Rising Second • Teacher's Edition   

# Drones

1   Did you see a flying craft that is not a <u>plane</u>? It could be a <u>drone</u>.

2   <u>Drones</u> are a fun fad for kids. A <u>drone</u> is <u>like</u> a <u>plane</u> but there is not a man

3   inside the craft. You <u>drive</u> a <u>drone</u> from a remote. Drones come in all

4   <u>sizes</u>. Some can be as big as a <u>plane</u>. Some are so little they can fit in

5   a hand.

6   A <u>drone</u> can see a lot. <u>Drones</u> can help cops when they spot a

7   <u>crime</u>. A <u>drone</u> cam can snap <u>live</u> film from over a big <u>game</u>. <u>Drones</u> can

8   help <u>save</u> a <u>life</u> too. They can fly a <u>drone</u> to <u>save</u> fish in the <u>lakes</u>. <u>Drones</u>

9   can find pipelines and see that they are in a <u>safe</u> state for <u>quite</u> some <u>time</u>.

10  If you get a new <u>drone</u>, spend <u>time</u> getting <u>used</u> to the <u>drone</u>. See

11  where you can fly it and how to get it back <u>home</u> when you fly it. It is not

12  fun to look for a missing <u>drone</u>.

13  There are online sites where you can get a lot of good facts on a

14  <u>drone</u>. You can <u>file</u> the best tips on how to fly and <u>use</u> a <u>drone</u>.

15  As one can see, there are lots of <u>uses</u> for <u>drones</u>. Kids <u>like</u> this fun

16  trend. If you <u>like</u> <u>planes</u>, <u>drone</u> flying will thrill you!

*Note:* Although the words *are, come, one, some, there,* and *where* appear to follow the long vowel silent-e pattern, these words do not have a long vowel sound.

| Long Vowel Silent-e | | | | | | Long Vowel Silent-e, Simple Multisyllable |
| --- | --- | --- | --- | --- | --- | --- |
| **Long a** | **Long e** | **Long i** | | **Long o** | **Long u** | |
| game | | crime | quite | drone | use | inside |
| lake | | drive | site | home | | online |
| plane | | file | size | | | pipeline |
| safe | | life | time | | | remote |
| save | | like | | | | |
| state | | live | | | | |

| Word Count* |
| --- |
| 227 |
| **Pattern Words** |
| 50 (22%) |
| * including title |

**Day 16**

# Days 16–20: Long Vowel Silent-e

## Learning Objective

In Days 16–20, students demonstrate understanding of the closed and long vowel silent-e patterns in both single and multisyllable words by correctly identifying, reading, and writing pattern words in isolation and in passages.

# DAY 16

## Phonological Awareness Warm-Up

**Today we are going to practice <u>adding a sound to the end</u> of a word. Let's review the instructions:**

- **I'll say a word and you repeat it.**
- **Next, I'll tell you what sound to add to the end of the word.**
- **Then, tell me the new word. Ready?**

| | | | |
|---|---|---|---|
| Say far: (**far**) Add /m/ to the end. Word? | **farm** | Say goal: (**goal**) Add /d/ to the end. Word? | **gold** |
| Say while: (**while**) Add /d/ to the end. Word? | **wild** | Say war: (**war**) Add /t/ to the end. Word? | **wart** |
| Say shell: (**shell**) Add /f/ to the end. Word? | **shelf** | Say ten: (**ten**) Add /t/ to the end. Word? | **tent** |
| Say fall: (**fall**) Add /t/ to the end. Word? | **fault** | Say hole: (**hole**) Add /d/ to the end. Word? | **hold** |
| Say mass: (**mass**) Add /k/ to the end. Word? | **mask** | Say lamb: (**lamb**) Add /p/ to the end. Word? | **lamp** |
| Say miss: (**miss**) Add /t/ to the end. Word? | **mist** | Say bill: (**bill**) Add /t/ to the end. Word? | **built** |
| Say class: (**class**) Add /p/ to the end. Word? | **clasp** | Say car: (**car**) Add /t/ to the end. Word? | **cart** |
| Say pass: (**pass**) Add /t/ to the end. Word? | **past** | Say coal: (**coal**) Add /d/ to the end. Word? | **cold** |

## Phonics Pattern

🔑 **Today we are reviewing words with the closed and long vowel silent-e patterns. Closed syllable words have 1 vowel letter followed by 1 or more consonants, and the vowel sound is short. Long vowel silent-e words have 1 vowel, 1 consonant, an e at the end, and the vowel sound is long.**

**Let's review.**

**What is the closed syllable pattern? Say it with me: Closed syllable words have 1 vowel letter followed by 1 or more consonants, and the vowel sound is short.**

**Gesture and say the syllable type.**  **closed**

**What is the long vowel silent-e syllable pattern? Say it with me: Long vowel silent-e words have 1 vowel, 1 consonant, an e at the end, and the vowel sound is long.**

**Gesture and say the syllable type.** **silent-e**

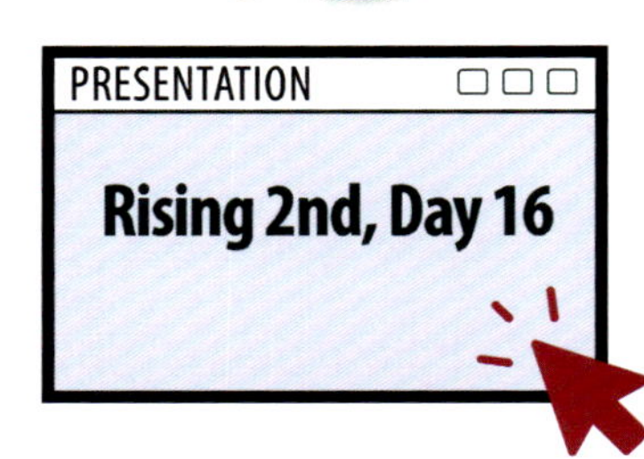

## SORT WORDS

(Display <u>lack</u>.)

 **I'm going to look for the closed or long vowel silent-e syllable patterns. Watch the steps I use:**

- **I find the vowel letter by pointing to it. There is 1 vowel letter followed by 2 consonants.**

- **This word HAS the closed syllable pattern. The vowel sound is /ă/.**

- **The gesture looks like this.** (Gesture and say "closed.")

- **I place the word in the closed column.** (Don't read the word yet)

**Let's sort the next word together. I'll answer and gesture with you.**
(Display <u>lake</u>.)

- **Look at this word. What do I do first?** find the vowel or vowels
  - **Yes, let's pretend to touch the vowel letter or letters.**

- **How many vowel letters?** 2

- **Syllable type and gesture?** long vowel silent-e

- **Vowel sound?** /ā/

- **Where does this word go?** in the long vowel silent-e column

 **Now it's your turn. Turn to page 28 in your Student Workbook. Decide if each word is a closed or a long vowel silent-e syllable. Then, write it in the correct column. Finally, read all the words in each column.**

### Answer Key

| Closed | Long Vowel Silent-e |
|---|---|
| lack | lake |
| slim | slime |
| cut | cute |
| back | bake |
| this | these |
| track | trade |
| not | note |

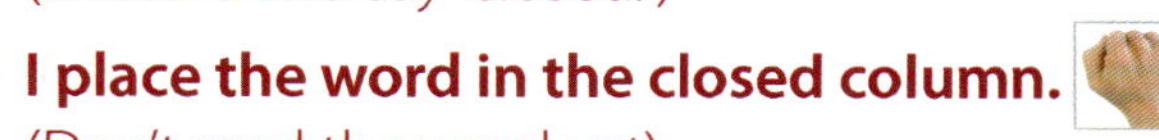

 **Routine for Word Sorting:**

- **Find the vowel or vowels.**
- **How many vowel letters?**
- **Syllable type and gesture?**
- **Vowel sound?**
- **Where does this word go?**
- **Read the words.**

1. slim
2. cut
3. slime
4. cute
5. bake
6. back
7. this
8. track
9. these
10. trade
11. note
12. not

 95 Phonics Booster Bundle™: Summer School Edition 2021 • Rising Second • Teacher's Edition **85**

**Day 16**

## Writing

### SOUND-SPELLING MAPPING WITH STUDENT PHONICS CHIPS

Now we're going to practice moving sound chips into boxes and then writing the letters to spell the words. Today we will add 2 new chips, a green sound chip and a green silent-e chip. The green chips represent a long vowel sound. Watch me decide whether I will use the red short vowel chip or the green long vowel chip.

The first word is <u>brave</u>.

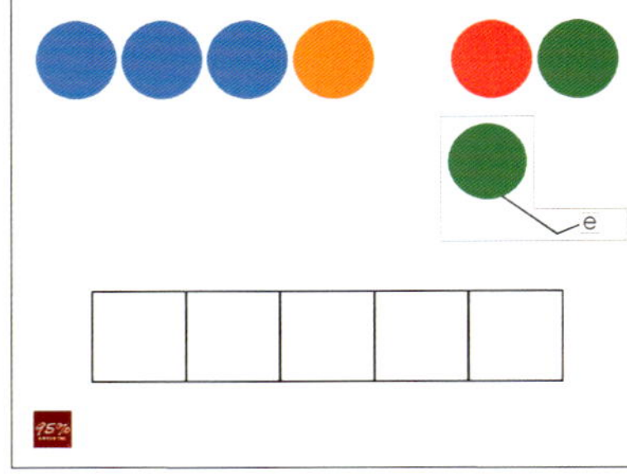

**Chips**

- First, I finger-stretch brave: /b/ /r/ /ā/ /v/.
- There are 4 sounds. I need 4 boxes for the 4 sounds. I place a dot in the bottom right corner of each box as I say the sounds. /b/ /r/ /ā/ /v/
- Now, I move chips into the boxes to represent the sounds.
  - The first sound is /b/. I pull down a blue chip.
  - The next sound is /r/. I pull down another blue chip.
  - The third sound is /ā/. This is a long vowel sound so I pull down the green chip.
  - The last sound is /v/. I pull down a blue chip.
- The sounds are /b/ /r/ /ā/ /v/. (Touch under each chip.)
- The word is brave. (Slide your finger under the word.)
- Since this word has the long vowel silent-e pattern, I replace the green sound chip with the green silent-e chip.

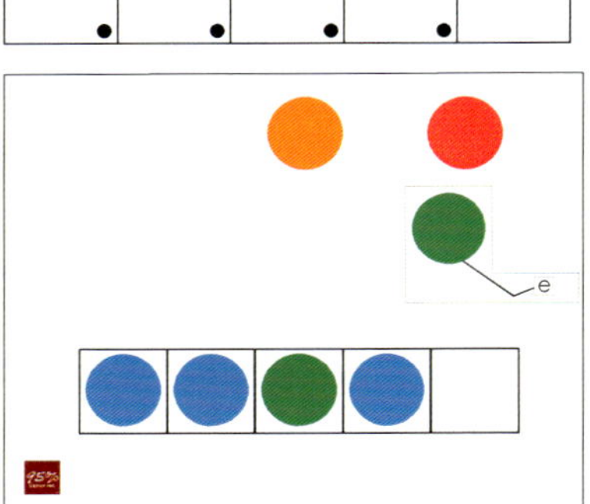

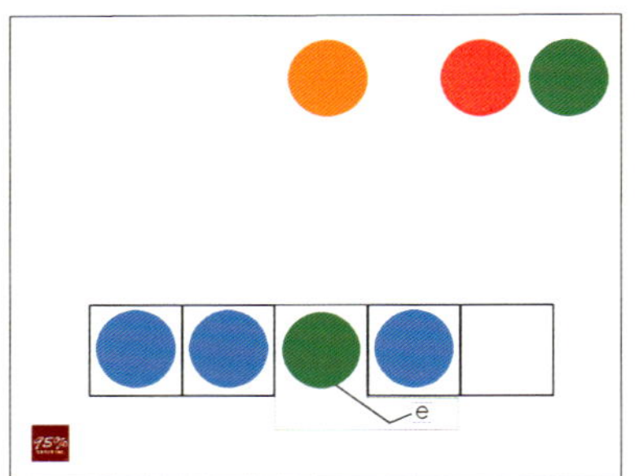

**Letters**

- Now, watch me write the letters that represent each sound.
  - The /b/ sound is spelled with the letter *b*. I write it in the first box.
  - The /r/ sound is spelled with the letter *r*. I write that in the second box.
  - The /ā/ sound is spelled with the letter *a* and a silent-e. I write the letter *a* in the third box and a small letter *e* in the corner of the fourth box. Since each box represents 1 sound, the silent-e does not get its own box because it does not make a sound. The silent-e shares a box with the next consonant.
  - The /v/ sound is spelled with the letter *v*. I write it in the fourth box.

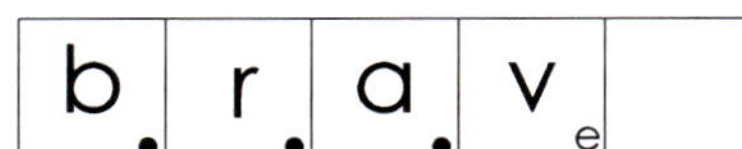

- **The word *brave* is a long vowel silent-e syllable.** (Make the silent-e syllable gesture under the word.)
    - **There is 1 vowel, 1 consonant, an e at the end, and the vowel sound is long.**
    - **Also, to show that the vowel *a* and the silent-e work together to make the long vowel sound, I draw a V-shape to connect the a and the silent-e.**
- **Let's review the sounds: /b/ /r/ /ā/ /v/.**
- **The word is brave.**

**Let's try the next word together. Watch me move the chips and write the letters.**

**The word is <u>slide</u>. Word? slide**

**Chips**
- **Finger-stretch slide. /s/ /l/ /ī/ /d/**
- **How many sounds? 4 How many boxes should I dot? 4**
- **First sound? /s/ Chip? blue**
- **Next sound? /l/ Chip? blue**
- **Next sound? /ī/ Is this a short or long vowel sound? long Chip? green**
- **Last sound? /d/ Chip? blue**
- **Sounds? /s/ /l/ /ī/ /d/ Word? slide**
- **Since this word has the long vowel silent-e pattern, let's change the green sound chip for the green silent-e chip.**

**Letters**
- **What letter spells the /s/ sound? s**
- **What letter spells the /l/ sound? l**
- **What letters spell the /ī/ sound? i and silent-e**
    - **I write the letter *i* in the third box and a small letter *e* in the corner of the fourth box.**
- **What letter spells the /d/ sound? d**
- **Is this a long vowel silent-e word? yes How do I mark the silent-e pattern? draw a V connecting the i and silent-e**
- **Sounds? /s/ /l/ /ī/ /d/**
- **Word? slide**

**Now it's your turn. Get your chips and mat ready. Remember to place the consonant chips on the left side, and the vowel chips on the right side. Lay out the following chips on your mat:**
- **3 blue chips**
- **1 orange chip**
- **1 red chip**
- **1 green chip**
- **1 green silent-e chip**

**Does your mat look like this?**

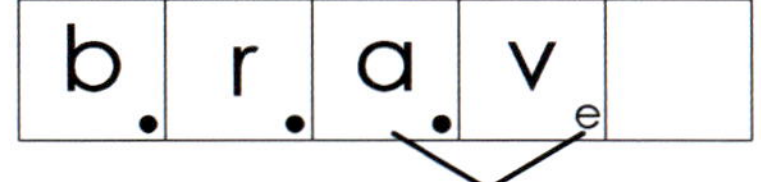

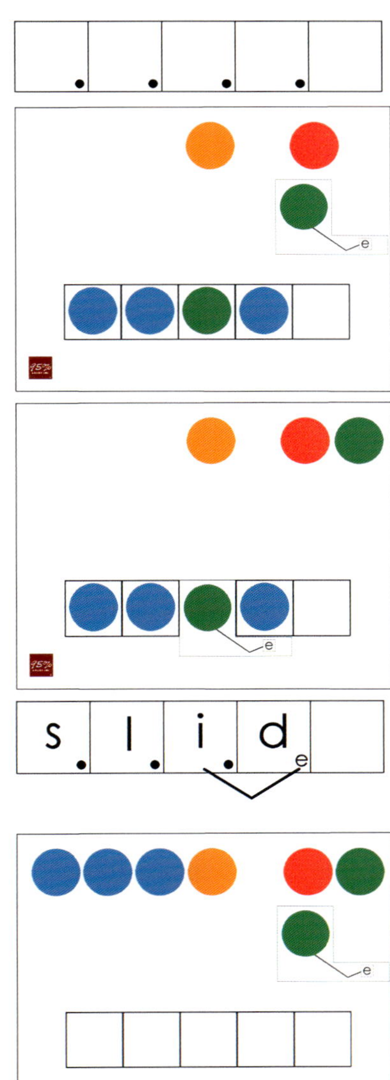

**Day 16**

 Now it's your turn. Turn to page 28 in your Student Workbook. Here are the steps:

1. I'm going to say a word and you'll repeat it.
2. Finger-stretch the sounds and place dots in your workbook.
3. Then, move chips on your mat.
4. Write the letters in your workbook.
5. Draw a V-shape connecting the vowels if the word follows the silent-e pattern.
6. Finally, whisper read the word.

**Routine for Chip Movement:**

- **Finger-stretch sounds.**
  - **How many sounds?**
  - **How many boxes?**
  - **Dot boxes in workbook.**
- **Sound? Chip?** (repeat for each sound)
- **Which letter spells the /_/ sound?** (repeat for each sound)
- **Word?**

**Answer Key**

| Words to Dictate | Placement of Phonics Chips on Mat | Correct Answers in Student Workbook |
|---|---|---|
| slide | 🔵🔵🟢🔵 ⌄e | s l i d e |
| 1. cake | 🔵🟢🔵 ⌄e | c a k e |
| 2. ship | 🟠🔴🔵 | sh i p |
| 3. twine | 🔵🔵🟢🔵 ⌄e | t w i n e |
| 4. globe | 🔵🔵🟢🔵 ⌄e | g l o b e |
| 5. drill | 🔵🔵🔴🔵 | d r i ll |

*Note:* The double consonant *l* in the word *drill* (#5) follows the Floss Rule. The double consonant makes 1 sound but is not considered a digraph. Double consonants are represented by a blue chip.

## Writing

### INFLECTED ENDINGS

Now, we will review the past tense ending *-ed*. Past tense is when a verb, which is an action word, changes to indicate that something happened in the past. The verb changes from present tense to past tense when the ending *-ed* is added.

There are 3 rules explaining how a spelling changes when the past tense *-ed* is added at the end of a verb. Let's review the 3 rules. (Display the Spelling Rules table.)

| Rule | Verb | Verb + ed | Spelling Rules |
|---|---|---|---|
| 1 | fish | fished | Verb spelled with a <u>vowel team, ends in y, or has 2 or more consonants at the end</u>, add -ed |
| 2 | bake | baked | Verb spelled with the <u>silent-e pattern, drop the last e</u> before adding -ed |
| 3 | tap | tapped | Verb spelled with <u>1 vowel followed by 1 consonant, the final consonant is doubled</u> before adding -ed |

Watch the steps I use to change a present tense verb to past tense by adding the past tense ending *-ed*.

**The verb is <u>like</u>.** (Display <u>like</u>.)

- First, I find the vowel or vowels and identify the syllable type.
  - The verb *like* has the long vowel silent-e pattern. It has the same syllable pattern as the verb *bake* in the table, which also has the long vowel silent-e pattern.

- The verb *like* ends in the letter *e*. Rule 2 is "drop the last e before adding -ed."

- I write the past tense verb *liked* in the "Verb + ed" column.

- Finally, I slide my finger under the past tense verb and whisper "liked."

| Verb | Verb + ed |
|------|-----------|
| like – rule 2 | liked |

 Now it's your turn. Turn to page 29 in your Student Workbook. Here are the steps:

1. Read each verb.
2. Find the vowels and identify the syllable type.
3. Decide which spelling rule fits the pattern and write the rule number next to the word in the first column.
4. Write the past tense verb in the "Verb + ed" column.
5. Whisper read the past tense verb.
6. Finally, choose 2 past tense verbs and write a sentence for each.

**Answer Key**

| Verb | Verb + ed |
|------|-----------|
| like – rule 2 | liked |
| 1. hike – rule 2 | hiked |
| 2. miss – rule 1 | missed |
| 3. chime – rule 2 | chimed |
| 4. stop – rule 3 | stopped |
| 5. help – rule 1 | helped |
| 6. grab – rule 3 | grabbed |

 

Day
**16**

## Passage Reading

### UNDERLINE/CIRCLE PATTERN WORDS

**Passage – Literary: *Jude's June Hike***

Now we'll practice finding 1- and 2-syllable words with the closed or long vowel silent-e patterns in a passage. Our passage today is about the surprise Jude had on her hike.

Today we are going to look for 1-syllable words containing the long vowel silent-e pattern and underline them. When we see a 2-syllable word with the closed or silent-e pattern, we will circle it. Then, we will sort the words into a chart.

**Let's look at the title of the passage.** (Do not read the title.) **The word *Jude's* follows the long vowel silent-e pattern, so I make the silent-e gesture, underline it, and write it in the long vowel silent-e column. Help me find more words. Remember we are looking for 1-syllable words with the silent-e pattern and 2-syllable words with closed and/or silent-e patterns. Hold up the appropriate syllable gesture or gestures when we come to a pattern word, and I'll underline or circle it. Then, we can decide where it belongs in our chart. Let's find 1 example of each type together.** (Continue underlining/circling pattern words to the black line.)

| Long Vowel Silent-e | Multisyllable |
| --- | --- |
| Jude | sunrise |

**Now it's your turn. Turn to page 30 in your Student Workbook. Here are the steps:**

1. **Begin at the black line and continue to the end of the passage.**
2. **Use your fingers to find the vowel or vowels.**
3. **Underline 1-syllable words with the silent-e pattern. Circle 2-syllable words with the closed and/or silent-e patterns.**
4. **Write the word in the correct column in the table under the passage on page 30. Continue until you find 5 more 1-syllable silent-e words and 3 more 2-syllable words. Don't list the same word more than once.**
5. **Finally, whisper read each word.**

(Refer to the note under the passage on page 82 for exceptions.)

**I'll give you a few minutes and then I will select a few students to share examples of words they identified and sorted.**

## Answer Key

| Long Vowel Silent-e | Multisyllable |
|---|---|
| Jude | sunrise |
| 1. (answers vary) | 1. inside |
| 2. | 2. homemade |
| 3. | 3. cupcakes |
| 4. | |
| 5. | |

***Note:*** When selecting students to share words they identified in the passage, ask which column they sorted each word into. Use the word table below the passage on page 82 to check the answers that students provide.

# DAY 17

## Phonological Awareness Warm-Up

**Today we are going to practice <u>adding a sound to the end</u> of a word.**
**Let's review the instructions:**
- **I'll say a word and you repeat it.**
- **Next, I'll tell you what sound to add to the end of the word.**
- **Then, tell me the new word. Ready?**

| | | | | |
|---|---|---|---|---|
| Say star: (**star**) Add /t/ to the end. Word? | **start** | Say bell: (**bell**) Add /t/ to the end. Word? | **belt** |
| Say four: (**four**) Add /k/ to the end. Word? | **fork** | Say guess: (**guess**) Add /t/ to the end. Word? | **guest** |
| Say an: (**an**) Add /t/ to the end. Word? | **ant** | Say miss: (**miss**) Add /t/ to the end. Word? | **mist** |
| Say fine: (**fine**) Add /d/ to the end. Word? | **find** | Say thumb: (**thumb**) Add /p/ to the end. Word? | **thump** |
| Say pain: (**pain**) Add /t/ to the end. Word? | **paint** | Say men: (**men**) Add /t/ to the end. Word? | **meant** |
| Say spill: (**spill**) Add /t/ to the end. Word? | **spilt** | Say win: (**win**) Add /d/ to the end. Word? | **wind** |
| Say pan: (**pan**) Add /t/ to the end. Word? | **pant** | Say plan: (**plan**) Add /t/ to the end. Word? | **plant** |
| Say hole: (**hole**) Add /d/ to the end. Word? | **hold** | Say mole: (**mole**) Add /d/ to the end. Word? | **mold** |

Day
17

## Phonics Pattern

### READING PATTERN WORDS

#### Review the Pattern

We're continuing to read and spell words with the closed and long vowel silent-e patterns.

Let's review the patterns for each syllable type.

**What is the closed syllable pattern? Say it with me:** Closed syllable words have 1 vowel letter followed by 1 or more consonants, and the vowel sound is short.

**Gesture and say the syllable type.** 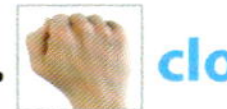 closed

**What is the long vowel silent-e syllable pattern? Say it with me:** Long vowel silent-e words have 1 vowel, 1 consonant, an e at the end, and the vowel sound is long.

**Gesture and say the syllable type.**  silent-e

#### Read Pattern Words

Now, we're going to read closed and silent-e syllable words.

When I show you a word, follow these steps:
1. Find the vowel or vowels and say the number of vowel letters.
2. Say the syllable type and show the gesture.
3. Say the vowel sound and keyword.
4. Read the word.

#### Answer Key

| Words on Presentation |
| --- |
| 1. (2, silent-e, /ō/ ocean) - home |
| 2. (2, silent-e, /ī/ ice) - crime |
| 3. (1, closed, /ă/ apple) - snack |
| 4. (2, silent-e, /ū/ unicorn) - tune |
| 5. (1, closed, /ŏ/ octopus) - slop |
| 6. (2, silent-e, /ī/ ice) - stripe |
| 7. (1, closed, /ŭ/ up) - jump |
| 8. (2, silent-e, /ō/ ocean) - rode |
| 9. (2, silent-e, /ā/ ape) - plate |
| 10. (2, silent-e, /ū/ Ruby) - cute |

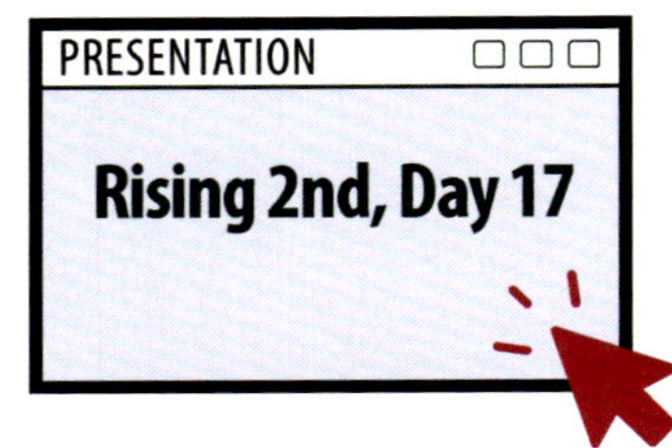


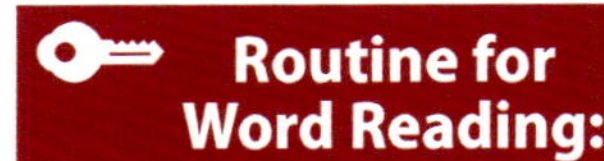


- Find the vowels.
- How many vowel letters?
- Syllable type and gesture?
- Vowel sound?
- Word?

| | |
| --- | --- |
| 1. home | 6. stripe |
| 2. crime | 7. jump |
| 3. snack | 8. rode |
| 4. tune | 9. plate |
| 5. slop | 10. cute |

## READING MULTISYLLABLE WORDS

**Now we will practice reading multisyllable words. Let me show you the routine.**

(Display reptile.)
**Here is the word.** (Do not read the word.)

**Step 1: Find the vowels.**
- I use both hands to find the vowels in each syllable.
- I point to the letter *e* with my left pointer finger and the letters *i* and *e* with my fingers in a V on my right hand.

**Step 2: Underline the vowels.**
- Next, I underline the vowels.
  - I underline the first e, the i, and the final e.
  - Also, since the second syllable has a silent-e pattern, I draw a V connecting the i and last e to show that these vowels work together.
- This word has 2 syllables because it has 2 vowel sounds.
  - The final-e is silent, so it does not count as a vowel sound.

**Step 3: Draw a line between the syllables.**
- I look for the number of consonants between the vowels.
- There are 2 — p and t. When there are 2 consonants between the 2 vowels, divide the word between them.
- I draw a syllable division line between the letters *p* and *t*.

**Step 4: Read each syllable.**

| Read the first syllable. | | Read the second syllable. | |
| --- | --- | --- | --- |
| I cover the second syllable and look at the first one. |  | I cover the first syllable and look at the second one. | |
| • The syllable type and gesture are closed.<br>• The vowel sound is /ĕ/.<br>• The syllable is rep. | | • The syllable type and gesture are silent-e.<br>• The vowel sound is /ī/.<br>• The syllable is tile. | |

**Step 5: Read the word.**
- The word is reptile.

**Day 17**

**Now, we will read some more multisyllable words using this routine. Let's do the first 2 together. Then, I will let you try some on your own.**
(Guide the students through the routine for reading the first 2 words; respond and gesture with them. Use a gradual release for the remaining 3 words.)

**When I show you a word, follow these steps:**
1. **Find the vowel or vowels and say the number of vowel sounds.**
2. **Say how many consonants are between the vowels.**
3. **Say where to divide the word.**
4. **Look at each syllable and do the following:**
   - **Say the syllable type and show the gesture.**
   - **Say the vowel sound.**
   - **Read the syllable.**
5. **Read the word.**

*Note:* Due to the multiple steps in this routine, prompt the students at each step. The Presentation file supports asking questions for each step. Use the "Routine for MS Word Reading" in the right margin to guide you.

> **Routine for MS Word Reading:**
> - **Find the vowels.** (2 hands)
> - **How many consonants between the vowels?**
> - **Where do I divide the syllables?**
> - **First syllable**
>   – Syllable type and gesture?
>   – Vowel sound?
>   – Syllable?
> - **Second syllable**
>   – Syllable type and gesture?
>   – Vowel sound?
>   – Syllable?
> - **Word?**

## Answer Key

| Word Number | # of Vowel Sounds | # of Cons. Between the Vowels | Division | First Syllable — Type | First Syllable — Sound | First Syllable — Read | Second Syllable — Type | Second Syllable — Sound | Second Syllable — Read | Word |
|---|---|---|---|---|---|---|---|---|---|---|
| 1. | 2 | 2 | in\|side | closed | /ĭ/ | in | silent-e | /ī/ | side | inside |
| 2. | 2 | 2 | cup\|cake | closed | /ŭ/ | cup | silent-e | /ā/ | cake | cupcake |
| 3. | 2 | 2 | on\|line | closed | /ŏ/ | on | silent-e | /ī/ | line | online |
| 4. | 2 | 1 | home\|made* | silent-e | /ō/ | home | silent-e | /ā/ | made | homemade |
| 5. | 2 | 2 | sun\|rise | closed | /ŭ/ | sun | silent-e | /ī/ | rise | sunrise |

*The word *homemade* is included in this activity to prepare the students for decoding the word in the passage. Since it does not have a simple syllable division, support students when dividing this word.

*Note:* Always encourage students to pretend to touch or point in the air at the vowel(s) and gesture when appropriate to maintain engagement. This is an overt method to check for understanding.

> 🍎 **Teacher Tip**
>
> If your students are struggling with the sections on multisyllable words, inflected endings, or contractions, consider spending more time on those sections.

Day
**17**

## Writing

### INFLECTED ENDINGS

**We practiced how to add the past tense ending -ed to a verb. Today we will learn the rules for adding 2 other endings to verbs: -ing and -s/-es. The rules are the same for adding -ing and -s/-es as for adding -ed. Let's review the 3 rules.**

(Display the <u>Spelling Rules</u> table. Read each spelling rule, and have the students chorally repeat it with you.)

| Rule | Verb | Verb + Ending | Spelling Rules |
|------|------|---------------|----------------|
| 1 | fish | fishing, fishes, fished | Verb spelled with a <u>vowel team, a y, or 2 or more consonants at the end,</u> add -ing, -es, or -ed. |
| 2 | bake | baking, bakes, baked | Verb spelled with the <u>silent-e pattern, drop the last e</u> before adding -ing, -es, or -ed. |
| 3 | tap | tapping, taps, tapped | Verb spelled with <u>1 vowel followed by 1 consonant, the final consonant is doubled</u> before adding -ing or -ed. For plurals, just add -s. |

**Watch what I do.**

(Display <u>dress</u>.)
**The verb is <u>dress</u>.**
- **First, I find the vowel or vowels and identify the syllable type.**
  - **The verb *dress* is a closed syllable with 2 consonants at the end.**
- **This verb has 2 consonants at the end, so I use rule 1 when I add the endings.**
- **I write the verbs *dresses*, *dressed*, and *dressing* in the correct columns.**
- **Finally, I whisper read each of the 3 verbs with the endings.**

| Verb | Verb + Ending | | |
|------|------|------|------|
| | s or es | ed | ing |
| dress – rule 1 | dresses | dressed | dressing |

**Now it's your turn. Turn to page 31 in your Student Workbook. Here are the steps:**

1. **Read the verb.**
2. **Find the vowel or vowels to identify the syllable type.**
3. **Decide which spelling rule fits the pattern and write the rule number next to word in the first column.**
4. **Write the verb with the endings -s or -es, -ed, and -ing.**
5. **Whisper read each of the verbs with the endings.**

**Day 17**

## Answer Key

| Verb | Verb + Ending | | |
|---|---|---|---|
| | s or es | ed | ing |
| dress – rule 1 | dresses | dressed | dressing |
| 1. bike – rule 2 | bikes | biked | biking |
| 2. plan – rule 3 | plans | planned | planning |
| 3. smile – rule 2 | smiles | smiled | smiling |
| 4. pinch – rule 1 | pinches | pinched | pinching |

## Writing

### WORD BUILDING

**We are going to practice changing words from the closed syllable pattern to the long vowel silent-e syllable pattern, or from long vowel silent-e to closed.**

(Display <u>bit</u>.)
**Watch me.**

- **The first word is spelled b-i-t.** (Do not read the word.)
  - **This word follows the closed syllable pattern because it has 1 vowel letter *i* followed by 1 consonant *t*. The vowel sound is short, /ĭ/.**
- **I write it in the closed syllable column and whisper read the word: *bit*.**
- **Now, I change the word *bit* to a long vowel silent-e pattern. I write the word *bit* in the long vowel silent-e column and add a silent-e to the end.**
- **The new word is spelled b-i-t-e.** (Do not read the word.) **The silent-e at the end changes the short vowel sound /ĭ/ to the long sound /ī/.**
- **Finally, I whisper read both words: *bit, bite*.**

**Now it's your turn. Turn to page 31 in your Student Workbook. Here are the steps:**

| Word | Closed | Long Vowel Silent-e |
|---|---|---|
| bit | bit | bite |

1. **Find the vowel or vowels to identify the syllable type.**
2. **Write the word in the closed or long vowel silent-e column.**
3. **Read the word.**
4. **Change the spelling of the word to fit the other pattern, and write it in the correct column.**
5. **Finally, whisper read both words.**

## Answer Key

| Word | Closed | Long Vowel Silent-e |
|---|---|---|
| bit | bit | bite |
| 1. cape | cap | cape |
| 2. theme | them | theme |
| 3. cop | cop | cope |
| 4. tube | tub | tube |
| 5. hope | hop | hope |

## Passage Reading

### READ PASSAGE

### Passage – Literary: *Jude's June Hike*

Now we'll read the passage. Today we're going to learn about Jude's surprise when she stops at her friend Pete's house. What do you think the surprise will be?

First, we'll read some of the underlined words together. When you see a word with a closed and/or silent-e syllable pattern, show me the appropriate syllable gesture with 1 or both hands and read the word. What is the first underlined or circled word? Jude's Read with me just the underlined and circled words above the black line.

 Now it's your turn. Turn to page 30 in your Student Workbook. Here are the steps:

1. First, whisper read all the underlined and circled words in the rest of the passage.
2. Then, go back to the beginning and whisper read the passage.

## Comprehension

### WRITTEN RESPONSE

In your Student Workbook, look at page 31. Complete the sentence about the passage. I'll give you a minute to do this, and then I'll ask for a couple of students to share what they wrote.

The note to Jude from Pete said ___________________________.
**(RL.1.1)** (come inside)

# DAY 18

## Phonological Awareness Warm-Up

Today we are going to practice <u>adding a sound to the end</u> of a word.
Let's review the instructions:
- I'll say a word and you repeat it.
- Next, I'll tell you what sound to add to the end of the word.
- Then, tell me the new word. Ready?

| | | | | |
|---|---|---|---|---|
| Say pass: (**pass**) Add /t/ to the end. Word? | **past** | Say while: (**while**) Add /d/ to the end. Word? | **wild** |
| Say mile: (**mile**) Add /d/ to the end. Word? | **mild** | Say sore: (**sore**) Add /t/ to the end. Word? | **sort** |
| Say when: (**when**) Add /t/ to the end. Word? | **went** | Say an: (**an**) Add /d/ to the end. Word? | **and** |
| Say car: (**car**) Add /t/ to the end. Word? | **cart** | Say plan: (**plan**) Add /t/ to the end. Word? | **plant** |
| Say run: (**run**) Add /t/ to the end. Word? | **runt** | Say star: (**star**) Add /t/ to the end. Word? | **start** |
| Say ram: (**ram**) Add /p/ to the end. Word? | **ramp** | Say miss: (**miss**) Add /t/ to the end. Word? | **mist** |
| Say win: (**win**) Add /d/ to the end. Word? | **wind** | Say six: (**six**) Add /th/ to the end. Word? | **sixth** |
| Say bun: (**bun**) Add /k/ to the end. Word? | **bunk** | Say in: (**in**) Add /ch/ to the end. Word? | **inch** |

## Phonics Pattern

### WORD READING ACCURACY

Look at the words. Let's read them together. As you read each word, hold up the closed or silent-e gesture. The bottom row has 2-syllable words. Don't forget to use 2 hands to gesture for each syllable.

| | | | |
|---|---|---|---|
| ride | quite | crane | these |
| shame | bent | fumes | joke |
| clap | those | drove | chant |
| smiles | crude | chime | liked |
| combine | magnet | picnic | dentist |

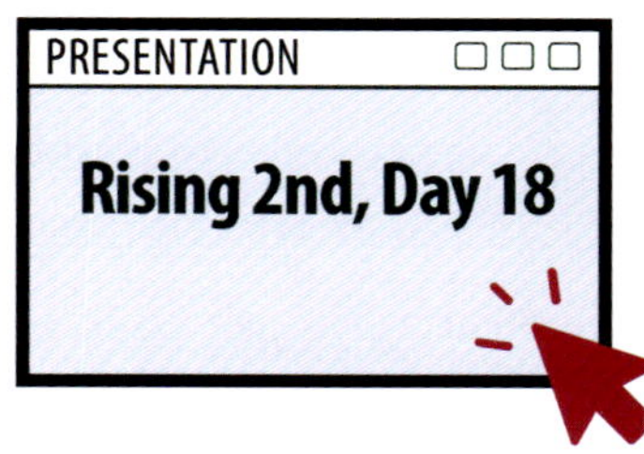


## Writing

### SYLLABLE MAPPING

Today we're going to practice spelling 2-syllable words with the closed and silent-e syllable patterns. Watch how I use the Syllable Mapping paper. Each box holds 1 syllable.

**The word is <u>mistake</u>.**
- **I tap one box for each syllable I hear: mis/take.** (With your hand under your chin, point out that it drops as you say each syllable.)
- **There are 2 syllables.**
- **Now, I write the letters that spell each syllable.**
  - **I write the first syllable, *mis*, in the first box: m-i-s.**
  - **I write the second syllable, *take*, in the second box: t-a-k-e.**
  - **I draw a V to connect the a and e since these vowels work together.**
- **The syllable types are closed and silent-e.** (Make the closed gesture with your left hand and the silent-e gesture with your right hand.)
- **I slide a finger under each syllable, combining them, and whisper "mistake."**

**Let's do one together.**

**The word is <u>homemade</u>. Word? homemade**
- **I tap each box while we say the syllables. home/made How many syllables? 2**

**Now, I write the letters that spell each syllable.**
- **First syllable? home**
  - **Sounds? /h/ /ō/ /m/**
  - **Letters? h-o-m-e I write it in the first box.**
  - **Syllable type and gesture?**  **silent-e How do I mark the silent-e pattern? draw a V connecting the o and e**
- **Second syllable? made**
  - **Sounds? /m/ /ā/ /d/ I write it in the second box.**
  - **Letters? m-a-d-e**
  - **Syllable type and gesture? silent-e How do I mark the silent-e pattern? draw a V connecting the a and e**
- **Word? homemade**

Now it's your turn. Turn to page 32 in your Student Workbook. Here are the steps:

1. **Say the word.**
2. **Tap a box for each syllable you hear.**
3. **For each syllable, say the sounds, write the letters, and say the syllable type while showing the gesture.**
4. **Mark a V connecting the vowels if the syllable follows the silent-e pattern.**
5. **Slide your finger under both syllables and whisper read the word to yourself.**

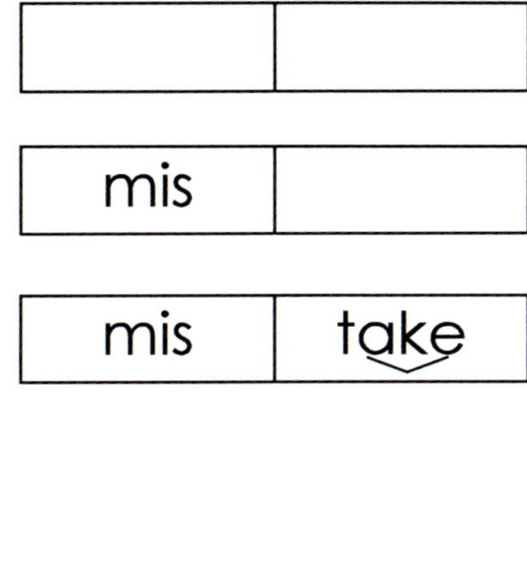

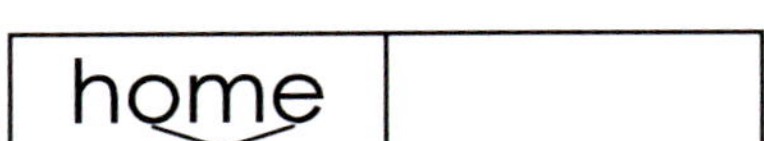

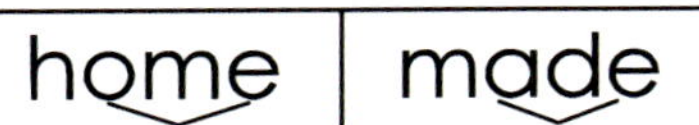

*Note:* Remind students that they can finger-stretch sounds to spell the syllables.

## Answer Key

| Words to Dictate | Correct Answers in Student Workbook | |
|---|---|---|
| homemade | home (silent-e) | made (silent-e) |
| 1. fitness | fit (closed) | ness (closed) |
| 2. sunshine | sun (closed) | shine (silent-e) |
| 3. pipeline | pipe (silent-e) | line (silent-e) |
| 4. basket | bas (closed) | ket (closed) |
| 5. invite | in (closed) | vite (silent-e) |

**Note:** Simple multisyllable words have 2 consonants between the vowel sounds. The words *sunshine* and *pipeline* do not follow this pattern but the students should be able to map them based on prior knowledge of the phonics patterns in both syllables (silent-e and consonant digraphs).

## Passage Reading

### READ PASSAGE

### Passage – Literary: *Jude's June Hike*

**Turn to page 30 in your Student Workbook. To build accuracy and fluency, you are going to practice reading *Jude's June Hike* again. While you're whisper reading about Jude and her friends, think about what is happening in the beginning, middle, and end of the passage.**

## Comprehension

### WRITTEN RESPONSE

**Now, turn to page 32 in your Student Workbook. Complete the graphic organizer at the bottom of the page. Write one complete sentence in each box telling what happened in the beginning, middle, and end of the passage. (RL.1.2)**

### Answer Key (answers vary)

| Beginning | Middle | End |
|---|---|---|
| Jude takes a 5-mile hike on her birthday to visit her pal Pete. | Jude stops by to see Pete and is surprised by her pals. | Jude and her pals have fun eating cupcakes and playing games. |

# DAY 19

## Phonological Awareness Warm-Up

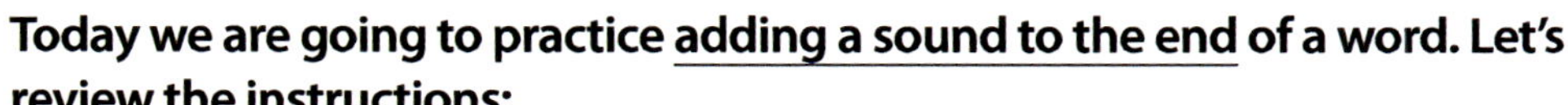

Today we are going to practice <u>adding a sound to the end</u> of a word. Let's review the instructions:

- I'll say a word and you repeat it.
- Next, I'll tell you what sound to add to the end of the word.
- Then, tell me the new word. Ready?

| | | | |
|---|---|---|---|
| Say see: (**see**) Add /t/ to the end. Word? | **seat** | Say were: (**were**) Add /k/ to the end. Word? | **work** |
| Say are: (**are**) Add /m/ to the end. Word? | **arm** | Say far: (**far**) Add /m/ to the end. Word? | **farm** |
| Say lamb: (**lamb**) Add /p/ to the end. Word? | **lamp** | Say pain: (**pain**) Add /t/ to the end. Word? | **paint** |
| Say wool: (**wool**) Add /f/ to the end. Word? | **wolf** | Say loss: (**loss**) Add /t/ to the end. Word? | **lost** |
| Say burn: (**burn**) Add /z/ to the end. Word? | **burns** | Say crow: (**crow**) Add /k/ to the end. Word? | **croak** |
| Say spy: (**spy**) Add /n/ to the end. Word? | **spine** | Say high: (**high**) Add /t/ to the end. Word? | **height** |
| Say tree: (**tree**) Add /t/ to the end. Word? | **treat** | Say wore: (**wore**) Add /n/ to the end. Word? | **warn** |
| Say while: (**while**) Add /d/ to the end. Word? | **wild** | Say true: (**true**) Add /th/ to the end. Word? | **truth** |

## Phonics Pattern

### SORT SYLLABLES

We have reviewed 2 of the 6 syllable types: closed and silent-e syllables. Today we are going to review another one—the open syllable. An open syllable has 1 vowel letter and no consonant letters after the vowel. We call this an open syllable because consonants do not "close in" the vowel. The vowel sound is long.

(Display <u>he</u>, <u>she</u>, and <u>me</u>.)
Look at these 3 words. These words are open syllables. These have 1 vowel letter followed by no consonants, and the vowel sound is long.

Repeat it with me: **Open syllables have 1 vowel letter followed by no consonants, and the vowel sound is long.**

The gesture for the open syllable is an open hand. 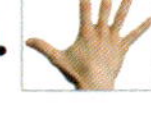
(Gesture and say "open.")

Let's practice identifying, sorting, and reading the syllables in multisyllable words. The syllables follow the closed, silent-e, and open syllable patterns. Watch me model with the first word.

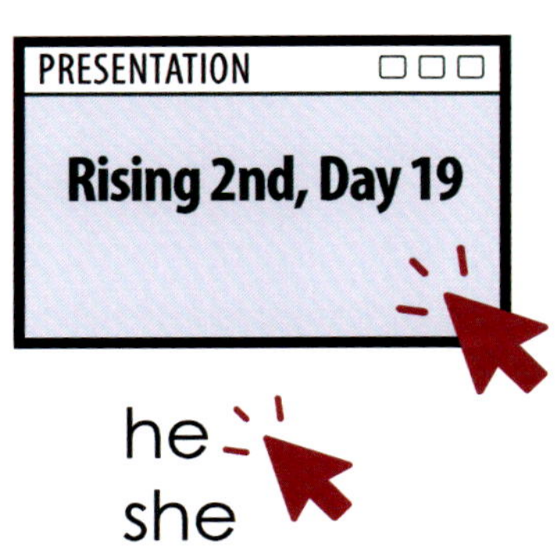

Day
19

(Display <u>remote</u>.)
**Here is the first word.** (Do not read the word.)

**Step 1: Find the vowels.**
- I use both hands to find the vowels in each syllable.
- I point to the first letter *e* with my left pointer finger, and the o and the last e with my fingers in the shape of a V on my right hand.
- There are 2 vowel sounds.

**Step 2: Underline the vowels.**
- Next, I underline the vowels.
  - I draw a V connecting the o and e to show they work together to make 1 sound.
- This word has 2 syllables because it has 2 vowel sounds.

**Step 3: Draw a line between the syllables.**
- I look for the number of consonants between the vowels.
- There is 1 consonant — m. Most often when there is 1 consonant between the vowel sounds, we divide before the consonant.
- I draw a syllable division line between the first e and the m.

**Step 4: Read and sort each syllable.**

| Sort the first syllable. | Sort the second syllable. |
|---|---|
| I cover the second syllable and look at the first one. 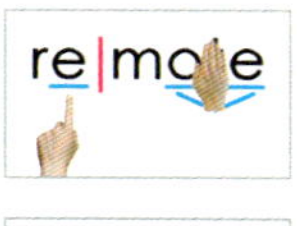<br>• The syllable type and gesture are open.<br>• The vowel sound is /ē/.<br>• The syllable is re. <br>I write the syllable *re* in the open syllable column. | I cover the first syllable and look at the second one.<br>• The syllable type and gesture are long vowel silent-e.<br>• The vowel sound is /ō/.<br>• The syllable is mote.<br>I write the syllable *mote* in the long vowel silent-e syllable column. |

**Step 5: Read the word.**
- The word is remote.

| Word | Closed | Long Vowel Silent-e | Open |
|---|---|---|---|
| re|mote | | mote | re |

**Now let's try one together. I'll answer and gesture with you.**
(Students should be pointing and gesturing throughout the routine.)

(Display <u>invite</u>.)
**Here is the word.** (Do not read the word.)

**Step 1: Find the vowels.**
- Use both hands to find the vowels in each syllable.
- Point to the first letter *i* with the left pointer finger, and the second letter *i* and the letter *e* with the right hand fingers in the shape of a V.
- How many vowel sounds? 2

**Step 2: Underline the vowels.**
- **Which letters should I underline to represent the vowel sounds?**
  **i, i, and e**
  - **How do I mark the silent-e? a V connecting the second i and e**
- **This word has 2 vowel sounds. How many syllables are there? 2**

invite

**Step 3: Draw a line between the syllables.**
- **How many consonants between the vowel sounds? 2**
- **Where do I draw a line? between the n and v**
- **I draw a syllable division line between the letters *n* and *v*.**

in|vite

**Step 4: Read and sort each syllable.**

<table>
<tr><td>

**Sort the first syllable.**

**I cover the second syllable and look at the first one.**
- **Syllable type and gesture? closed**
- **Vowel sound? /ĭ/**
- **Syllable? in**
- **Where do I write the syllable *in*? closed syllable column**

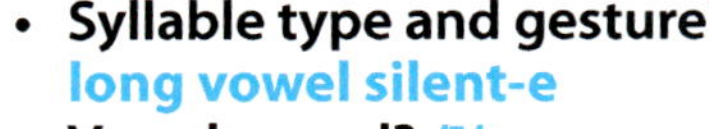

</td><td>

**Sort the second syllable.**

**I cover the first syllable and look at the second one.**
- **Syllable type and gesture? long vowel silent-e**
- **Vowel sound? /ī/**
- **Syllable? vite**
- **Where do I write the syllable *vite*? long vowel silent-e syllable column**

</td></tr>
</table>

**Step 5: Read the word.**
- **Word? invite**

| Word | Closed | Long Vowel Silent-e | Open |
|------|--------|---------------------|------|
| in\|vite | in | vite | |

**Now it's your turn. Turn to page 33 in your Student Workbook. Here are the steps:**

1. **Find the vowels and underline them.**
2. **Count the consonants between the vowels. Remember, if there is 1 consonant between the vowel sounds, divide before the consonant.**
3. **Draw a line between the syllables.**
4. **Sort each syllable.**
   - **Say the syllable type and show the gesture.**
   - **Say the vowel sound and read the syllable.**
   - **Write the syllable in the correct column.**
5. **Read the word.**

**I'll check back with you in a few minutes and then you can check your answers.**

## Answer Key

| Word | Closed | Long Vowel Silent-e | Open |
|------|--------|---------------------|------|
| in\|vite | in | vite | |
| 1. on\|line | on | line | |
| 2. pub\|lic | pub    lic | | |
| 3. si\|ren | ren | | si |
| 4. web\|site | web | site | |
| 5. in\|vade | in | vade | |
| 6. fro\|zen | zen | | fro |
| 7. es\|cape | es | cape | |
| 8. ro\|bot | bot | | ro |

## Writing

## CONTRACTIONS

Today we will read and write more contractions. Remember, contractions occur when 2 words are put together and shortened into 1 word. An apostrophe is used to show where a letter or letters are dropped when 2 words are combined. Read these contractions with me:

(Display contractions.)

- **don't**
- **isn't**
- **hasn't**
- **can't**

**Which two words make up the contraction** *don't*? do not **Which letter is dropped?** the second o

(Display sentence.)
**Read this sentence with me.** I don't like to rest.

**Let's try another one.**

(Display let's.)
**The contraction is** let's.

- **Which word do you recognize in this contraction?** let
- **Yes, this contraction is made up of the words** *let* **and** *us* **combined and shortened by removing 1 letter.**
- *Let's* **means the same thing as** *let us*; **it is just a shortened way to use those words in our writing and speaking.**
- **In the contraction** *let's*, **which letter or letters have been replaced with an apostrophe?** u
  - Yes, the u is dropped.
- **Spell the contraction** *let's* **with me. Don't forget to say "apostrophe."** l-e-t-apostrophe-s
- **Word?** let's



 95 Phonics Booster Bundle™: Summer School Edition 2021 • Rising Second • Teacher's Edition

**Now it's your turn. Turn to page 33 in your Student Workbook. Here are the steps:**

1. **Look at the 2 words in the first column.**
2. **Combine them in the middle column.**
3. **Draw a slash through the letter or letters to be removed.**
4. **Then, write the new word with the apostrophe replacing the slashed letters in the last column.**
5. **Whisper read the contraction to yourself.**
6. **Finally, orally share with a partner a sentence using 1 of the contractions.**

### Answer Key

| 2 Words | Combine Words and Slash | Contraction |
|---|---|---|
| let us | let**u̸s** | let's |
| 1. can not | can**n̸o̸t** | can't |
| 2. is not | is**n̸o̸t** | isn't |
| 3. I am | I**a̸m** | I'm |
| 4. it is | it**i̸s** | it's |
| 5. did not | did**n̸o̸t** | didn't |

## Passage Reading

### READ PASSAGE

### Passage – Informational: *Drones*

**Now it's time to read a new passage. This passage will give us information about drones. Do you know what a drone is?**

**Turn to page 34 in your Student Workbook. We will read the passage *Drones* as a class. We will use a new strategy for reading today—oral cloze reading. I will read the passage to the black line and pause at the silent-e and 2-syllable pattern words that are already underlined and circled in your workbook. When I pause, you will chorally read the word that comes next. It is important you are following along as I read so you will be able to respond when needed.** (Model fluency while reading the passage and pause at the underlined and circled words. Stop at the black line.)

**You will read the rest of the passage independently. While you are reading, think about the main topic and key details in the passage.**

***Note:*** Oral cloze reading is a strategy used to model fluency and increase engagement.

Day
**19**

## Comprehension

### WRITTEN RESPONSE

**Turn to page 35 in your Student Workbook. Let's talk about the main topic and key details of this passage.** (Guide the students in discussion and completion of the graphic organizer.) **(RI.1.2)**

- **Let's begin by writing the title of the passage at the top of the graphic organizer. What is the title of the passage? Drones**
  - **Don't forget that the letter _D_ in _Drones_ needs to be capitalized because it is a title.**

| **Title:** Drones |
| --- |

- **What is the main topic of this passage? Remember, the main topic answers the question, "What is this passage mostly about?"** (answers vary: what drones do, what we use them for, how they are helpful)

  - **Write, "Drones are helpful in many ways." as the main topic in your graphic organizer.**

| Main Topic |
| --- |
| Drones are helpful in many ways. |

*Note:* Give students an opportunity to share their idea with a partner or as a class.

- **What are some things that we learned drones can do?**
  (answers vary: spot crime, snap live film, save fish, find pipelines)

  - **Choose 3 of the details to write in your graphic organizer. Make sure to use complete sentences with a capital at the beginning and correct punctuation at the end.**

*Note:* Post student responses on chart paper or a whiteboard. Students can refer to this when completing the Key Details portion of the graphic organizer.

### Answer Key

| **Title:** Drones |
| --- |
| **Main Topic** |
| Drones are helpful in many ways. |
| **Key Details** |
| 1. Drones can spot crime. |
| 2. Drones can film games. |
| 3. Drones can be used to save a life. |

(Answers for the key details will vary.)

# DAY 20

## Phonological Awareness Warm-Up

Today we are going to practice <u>adding a sound to the end</u> of a word. Let's review the instructions:
- I'll say a word and you repeat it.
- Next, I'll tell you what sound to add to the end of the word.
- Then, tell me the new word. Ready?

| | | | | |
|---|---|---|---|---|
| Say tea: (tea) Add /ch/ to the end. Word? | **teach** | Say four: (four) Add /t/ to the end. Word? | **fort** |
| Say are: (are) Add /t/ to the end. Word? | **art** | Say bun: (bun) Add /t/ to the end. Word? | **bunt** |
| Say hum: (hum) Add /p/ to the end. Word? | **hump** | Say car: (car) Add /d/ to the end. Word? | **card** |
| Say fill: (fill) Add /d/ to the end. Word? | **filled** | Say lie: (lie) Add /t/ to the end. Word? | **light** |
| Say loss: (loss) Add /t/ to the end. Word? | **lost** | Say ban: (ban) Add /d/ to the end. Word? | **band** |
| Say hall: (hall) Add /t/ to the end. Word? | **halt** | Say her: (her) Add /t/ to the end. Word? | **hurt** |
| Say store: (store) Add /m/ to the end. Word? | **storm** | Say core: (core) Add /d/ to the end. Word? | **cord** |
| Say shell: (shell) Add /f/ to the end. Word? | **shelf** | Say den: (den) Add /t/ to the end. Word? | **dent** |

## Writing

### SYLLABLE MAPPING

Today we're going to practice spelling 2-syllable words with closed and silent-e syllables.

We have done this before. We will use the Syllable Mapping paper. Remember, each box holds 1 syllable.

Let's do one together.

The first word is <u>tadpole</u>. Word? **tadpole**
- I tap each box while we say the syllables. **tad/pole** How many syllables? **2**
- Now, I write the letters that spell each syllable.
- First syllable? **tad**
  - Sounds? **/t/ /ă/ /d/**
  - Letters? **t-a-d** I write them in the first box.
  - Syllable type and gesture?  **closed**
- Second syllable? **pole**
  - Sounds? **/p/ /ō/ /l/**
  - Letters? **p-o-l-e** I write them in the second box.
  - Syllable type and gesture? **silent-e** How do I mark the silent-e pattern? **draw a V connecting the o and e**
- Word? **tadpole**

PRESENTATION

**Rising 2nd, Day 20**

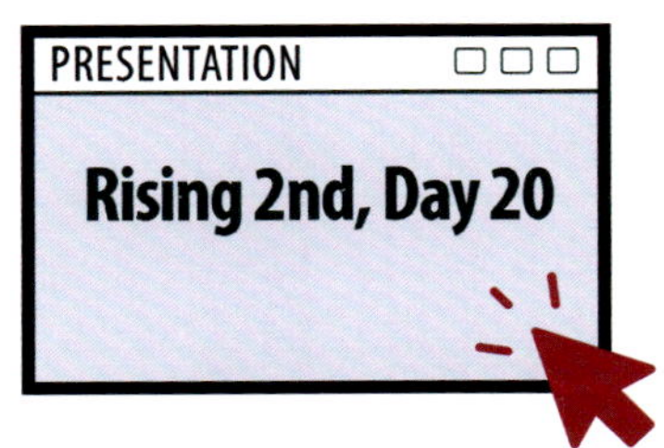
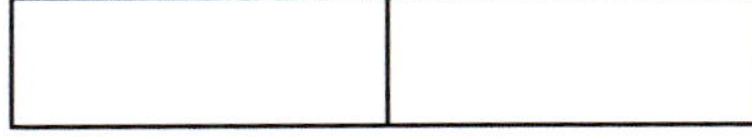

| tad | |

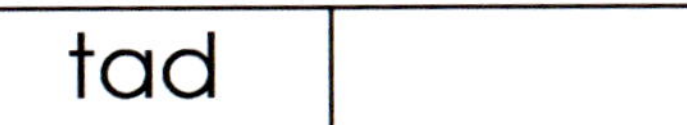

| tad | pole |

**Day 20**

**Now it's your turn. Turn to page 35 in your Student Workbook. Here are the steps:**

1. Say the word.
2. Tap a box for each syllable you hear.
3. For each syllable, say the sounds, write the letters, and say the syllable type while showing the gesture.
4. Mark a V connecting the vowels if the syllable follows the silent-e pattern.
5. Slide your finger under both syllables and whisper read the word to yourself.

**Answer Key**

| Words to Dictate | Correct Answers in Student Workbook | |
| --- | --- | --- |
| tadpole | tad (closed) | pole (silent-e) |
| 1. upset | up (closed) | set (closed) |
| 2. hotdog | hot (closed) | dog (closed) |
| 3. compete | com (closed) | pete (silent-e) |
| 4. escape | es (closed) | cape (silent-e) |
| 5. button | but (closed) | ton (closed) |

*Note:* Remind students that they can finger-stretch sounds to spell the syllables.

*Note:* The first syllable in the word *compete* (#3) and the second syllable in the word *button* (#5) have the schwa sound. Point this out to the students and guide them in spelling these syllables correctly.

## Writing

### WORD BUILDING

Today you will build 2-syllable words by choosing 2 syllables from a Syllable Bank and putting them together.

Watch the steps I use:
- I choose 2 syllables from the Syllable Bank. I take the syllable *ex* from the closed column and the syllable *plode* from the silent-e column.
- I write the new word *explode* in the Multisyllable Words table.
- Now, I read the word *explode*.

| Multisyllable Words |
| --- |
| explode |

**Now it's your turn. Turn to page 36 in your Student Workbook. Here are the steps:**

1. Choose 2 syllables from the Syllable Bank.
2. Read each syllable. Blend the syllables and read the word.
3. If this is not a word you know, try different syllables.
4. Write the multisyllable word, and then whisper read it.
5. Repeat until you have built 4 multisyllable words.

You can use the syllables more than once when building words.

| Syllable Bank | |
| --- | --- |
| **Closed** | **Silent-e** |
| ex | bone |
| back | plode |
| lunch | made |
| pack | home |
| box | line |
| in | lime |
| put | side |
| on | ade |
| hand | shake |

## Answer Key

| Multisyllable Words | |
| --- | --- |
| explode | backbone |
| inside | lunchbox |
| limeade | backpack |
| input | homemade |
| online | handshake |

*Note:* The Answer Key includes many, but not all, of the possible words.

*Note:* As a strategy for adding engagement or to scaffold this activity, you can have groups or pairs of students put these syllables on index cards or sticky notes. Students can collaborate while manipulating the syllables to build words.

## Fluency

### PHRASES

**Today you are going to read phrases from the passage. You will notice there are slashes between sets of words. The slashes are there to divide the text into phrases. Phrase reading will help build fluency and comprehension of the text you are reading. Let's read some phrases from the passage *Drones* together.**

(Display paragraph from *Drones*.)

> **Did you see/ a flying craft/ that is not/ a plane?/ It could be/ a drone./ Drones are/ a fun fad/ for kids./ A drone/ is like/ a plane/ but there is not/ a man inside/ the craft.**

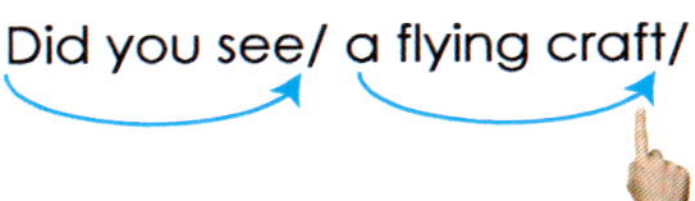



*Note:* Model how to use your finger to scoop under the phrases as you read.

**Day 20**

**Now it's your turn. Turn to page 36 in your Student Workbook. When I say "begin," point to the first phrase and whisper it. Continue reading across the page. If you finish before I say "stop," start at the top and read the phrases again.** (Time students for 1 minute. Say "stop" and ask students to circle the last phrase that was read.)

A drone/ can see/ a lot./ Drones can/ help cops/ when they spot/ a crime./ A drone cam/ can snap/ live film/ from over/ a big game./ Drones can help save/ a life too./ They can fly/ a drone/ to save fish/ in the lakes./ Drones can/ find pipelines/ and see/ that they/ are in/ a safe state/ for quite some time./

## Writing

### SENTENCE WRITING

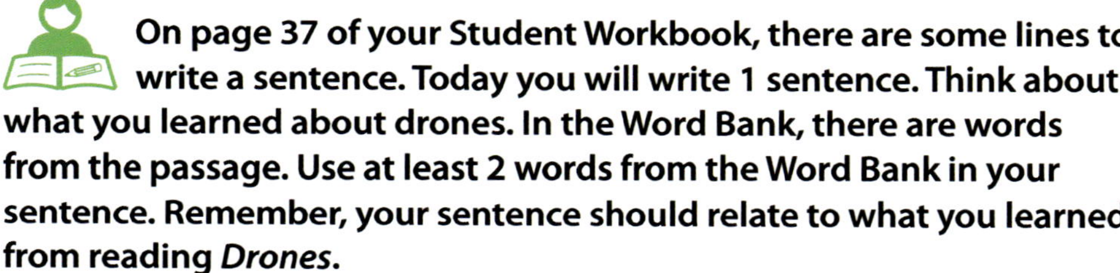

**On page 37 of your Student Workbook, there are some lines to write a sentence. Today you will write 1 sentence. Think about what you learned about drones. In the Word Bank, there are words from the passage. Use at least 2 words from the Word Bank in your sentence. Remember, your sentence should relate to what you learned from reading** *Drones*.

| Word Bank | | | | |
|---|---|---|---|---|
| safe | cute | game | life | plane |
| save | size | drone | time | lake |
| like | use | home | excite | drive |

(answers vary: Check for complete sentences and relevance to the topic.)

## Passage Reading

### READ PASSAGES

Today you are going to practice reading both of the passages. One was about a surprise birthday party. The second was about how drones can be helpful.

## Comprehension

### WRITTEN RESPONSE

Turn to page 37 in your Student Workbook. Read both passages, then write the answer to the question for each passage in your workbook.

Passage – Literary: *Jude's June Hike* on page 30
1. Jude was glad to see her pals. What was a time when you were glad to see pals? **(RL.1.3)** (answers vary)

Passage – Informational: *Drones* on page 34
1. How could Jude, from *Jude's June Hike*, use a drone on her hike? **(RI.1.3)** (answers vary)

### Teacher Tip

Have you observed students who can read a word in isolation and then can't successfully read it in a passage? This program uses a unique process to help students bridge from learning to read words containing the phonics pattern to fluently reading them within connected text. It's called "transfer to text" and it involves scaffolding from finding and underlining the pattern words to then practicing them first before reading the text. This leads to improved proficiency in reading them in connected text.

 

# The Rascal

1  Justin and I went to Griffin's home to plant seeds in his yard. We hoped to
2  have a picnic after that. Griffin had just locked Bandit's leash to the sundeck.
3  Bandit, Griffin's basset dog, often finds problems. I asked Griffin what Bandit did
4  to be stuck on the sundeck. He pointed to piles of messed up soil in his yard. He
5  looked up at the frantic dog and said, "I think the hound dug that hole in the dirt.
6  Bandit has dirt all over the yard and me too!"
7  We went to work planting seeds. "See that?" Griffin said as he pointed to a
8  ripped seed packet. We stopped planting to check out the problem. The seeds
9  were in a pile. "Griffin, you have to admit this is not Bandit's work," Justin said.
10  "We can dismiss Bandit as the rascal."
11  "See this hole next to the seed packet?" I asked. "What could be in that
12  tunnel?" Griffin was going to find what was hidden there. All of a sudden, he
13  rushed into the shed. He was missing for a short time, and then came back with a
14  wire box. Griffin said not to be upset. It was a box to trap the rascal. Griffin's plan
15  was to catch the rascal and set him free, far away from the plants.
16  We put walnuts in the box to set a trap for the rascal. We undid Bandit's
17  leash and went inside to wait. After a short time, Griffin looked and said, "We got
18  him!" The rascal turned out to be a chipmunk! He was cute, but Griffin said he
19  was a problem and had to go. Justin set the chipmunk free. At last, we can enjoy
20  our picnic!

| Simple Multisyllable Words | | | |
|---|---|---|---|
| admit | frantic | packet | tunnel |
| Bandit | Griffin | picnic | undid |
| basset | hidden | problem | upset |
| chipmunk | inside | rascal | walnut |
| dismiss | Justin | sudden | |
| enjoy | often | sundeck | |

| Word Count* |
|---|
| 290 |
| **Pattern Words** |
| 51 (18%) |

* including title

# Sundecks

1  A sundeck is a spot to lay in the sun and let the sunrays warm the skin.
2  All sundecks are sunlit and can be found on the upper deck of a ship, on a
3  boat, or at a home. At home, in a boat, or on a ship, you can have a picnic
4  on a sundeck. It is a perfect spot to eat lunch or dinner. At home, you can
5  invite pals to a picnic.

6  A sundeck on the top deck of a ship can go round the entire upper
7  deck. If the ship is big, there are spots for lots of chairs and hammocks to lay
8  upon in the sun. There are plastic chairs and cloth hammocks on sundecks
9  for the crowd to enjoy the sunrays. There are also rustic chairs and hammocks
10  too. It is safe to rest on a sundeck when the ship is under way.

11  Small boats have sundecks too. The best spot for a sundeck on a little
12  boat is at the rear. The small size of the boat means the sundeck has a spot
13  for just one person at a time.

14  A sundeck can be part of a home. It's like a porch at the back of a
15  home. If the sundeck is old and dark, you can update it with some pastel
16  paint or fresh stain. You might put plastic chairs and a hammock there too.

17  In the winter, a sundeck is still fun to warm up in the sun, but sundecks
18  are used most often in the fall, spring, and summer. Keep a basket of cream
19  to get a suntan and not a sunburn. If you have a sundeck, you will want to
20  enjoy the sunrays with pals.

| Simple Multisyllable Words | | | | Word Count* |
|---|---|---|---|---|
| basket | often | rustic | suntan | 288 |
| dinner | pastel | summer | under | **Pattern Words** |
| enjoy | perfect | sunburn | update | 46 (16%) |
| entire | person | sundeck | upon | * including title |
| hammock | picnic | sunlit | upper | |
| invite | plastic | sunray | winter | |

**Day 21**

# Days 21–25: Closed, Simple Multisyllable

## Learning Objective

In Days 21–25, students demonstrate proficiency with simple, closed-closed multisyllable words and an understanding of multisyllable words with silent-e, vowel team, and vowel-r syllables by correctly identifying, reading, and writing pattern words in isolation and in passages.

# DAY 21

## Phonological Awareness Warm-Up

**Today we are going to practice <u>substituting, or changing, the vowel sound</u> in a word. Let's review the instructions:**
- **I'll say a word and you repeat it.**
- **Next, I'll tell you what sound to substitute, or change, in the word.**
- **Then, tell me the new word. Ready?**

| | | | |
|---|---|---|---|
| Say bad: (**bad**) Change /ă/ to /ĕ/. Word? | **bed** | Say lake: (**lake**) Change /ā/ to /ē/. Word? | **leak** |
| Say six: (**six**) Change /ĭ/ to /ŏ/. Word? | **socks** | Say hope: (**hope**) Change /ō/ to /ŏ/. Word? | **hop** |
| Say feel: (**feel**) Change /ē/ to /ĕ/. Word? | **fell** | Say hid: (**hid**) Change /ĭ/ to /ă/. Word? | **had** |
| Say soup: (**soup**) Change /ū/ to /ĭ/. Word? | **sip** | Say cop: (**cop**) Change /ŏ/ to /ă/. Word? | **cap** |
| Say bell: (**bell**) Change /ĕ/ to /ĭ/. Word? | **bill** | Say lift: (**lift**) Change /ĭ/ to /ĕ/. Word? | **left** |
| Say pan: (**pan**) Change /ă/ to /ĕ/. Word? | **pen** | Say fan: (**fan**) Change /ă/ to /ĭ/. Word? | **fin** |
| Say crib: (**crib**) Change /ĭ/ to /ă/. Word? | **crab** | Say net: (**net**) Change /ĕ/ to /ŏ/. Word? | **not** |
| Say peel: (**peel**) Change /ē/ to /ĭ/. Word? | **pill** | Say band: (**band**) Change /ă/ to /ĕ/. Word? | **bend** |

## Phonics Pattern

Today we will practice reading, spelling, and dividing simple multisyllable words that follow the closed-closed syllable pattern. A word with the closed-closed pattern has 2 syllables and both syllables follow the closed syllable pattern. Each syllable will have 1 vowel sound. There will be 2 consonants between the vowel sounds; we usually divide between them.

**Repeat it with me: Every syllable must have a vowel sound. When there are 2 consonants between the vowel sounds, we usually divide between them.**

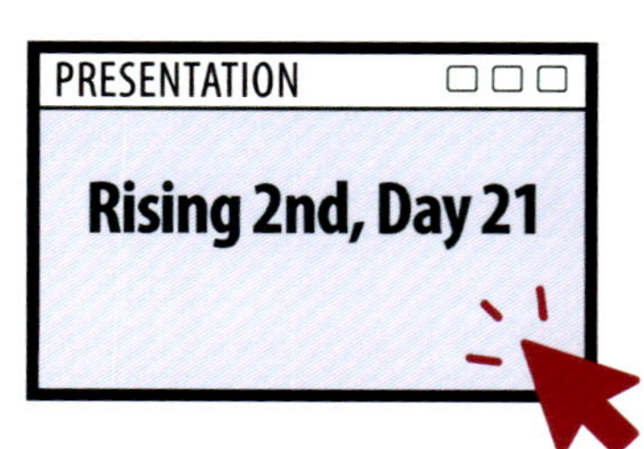

## READING MULTISYLLABLE WORDS

Let's review the routine for reading multisyllable words.

(Display basket.)
**Here is the word.** (Do not read the word.)

**Step 1: Find the vowels.**
- **I use both hands to find the vowels in each syllable.**
- **I point to the letter *a* with my left pointer finger and the letter *e* with my right pointer finger.**
- **There are 2 vowel sounds.**

**Step 2: Underline the vowels.**
- **Next, I underline the vowels.**
- **This word has 2 syllables because it has 2 vowel sounds.**



**Step 3: Draw a line between the syllables.**
- **I look for the number of consonants between the vowels.**
- **There are 2 — s and k. When there are 2 consonants between the 2 vowels, divide the word between them.**
- **I draw a syllable division line between the letters *s* and *k*.**



**Step 4: Read each syllable.**

<table>
<tr><td>

**Read the first syllable.**

**I cover the second syllable and look at the first one.**
- **The syllable type and gesture are closed.**
- **The vowel sound is /ă/.**
- **The syllable is bas.**

</td><td>

</td><td>

**Read the second syllable.**

**I cover the first syllable and look at the second one.**
- **The syllable type and gesture are closed.**
- **The vowel sound is /ĕ/.**
- **The syllable is ket.**

</td><td>




</td></tr>
</table>

**Step 5: Read the word.**
- **The word is basket.**

**Now we'll read another multisyllable word together. When I show you the word, I'll answer and gesture with you.** (Students should be pointing and gesturing throughout the routine.)

(Display subject.)
**Here is the word.** (Do not read the word.)

**Step 1: Find the vowels.**
- **Use both hands to find the vowels in each syllable.**
- **Point to the letter *u* with the left pointer finger and the letter *e* with the right pointer finger.**
- **How many vowel sounds? 2**

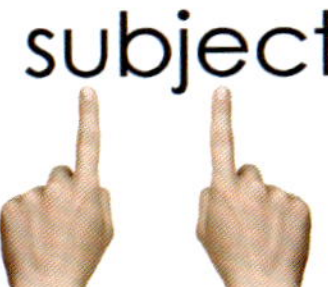


**Step 2: Underline the vowels.**
- **Next, we underline the vowels.**
- **This word has 2 vowel sounds. How many syllables? 2**

**Step 3:** Draw a line between the syllables.
- How many consonants between the 2 vowel sounds? **2**
- Where do I draw the line? **between the b and j**
- We draw a syllable division line between the letters *b* and *j*.

sub|ject

**Step 4:** Read each syllable.

| | |
|---|---|
| **Read the first syllable.**<br>Cover the second syllable and look at the first one. <br>• Syllable type? **closed**<br>• Vowel sound? **/ŭ/**<br>• Syllable? **sub** | **Read the second syllable.**<br>Cover the first syllable and look at the second one. <br>• Syllable type? **closed**<br>• Vowel sound? **/ĕ/**<br>• Syllable? **ject** |

**Step 5:** Read the word.
- Word? **subject**

 Now it's your turn. Turn to page 38 in your Student Workbook. Here are the steps:

1. Find the vowels and underline them.
2. Count the consonants between the vowel sounds and draw a line between them.
3. For each syllable:
   - Say the syllable type.
   - Say the vowel sound.
   - Read the syllable.
4. Read the word.

**Answer Key**

| | | |
|---|---|---|
| sub\|ject | 3. hel\|met | 6. in\|dex |
| 1. ten\|nis | 4. un\|til | 7. fit\|ness |
| 2. mag\|net | 5. hid\|den | 8. den\|tist |

**Routine for MS Word Reading:**
- Underline the vowels.
- How many consonants between the vowels?
- Where do I divide the syllables?
- First syllable
  - Syllable type and gesture?
  - Vowel sound?
  - Syllable?
- Second syllable
  - Syllable type and gesture?
  - Vowel sound?
  - Syllable?
- Word?

## Writing

### SYLLABLE MAPPING

Today we're going to practice spelling multisyllable words with the closed-closed syllable pattern. Watch how I use the Syllable Mapping paper. Each box holds 1 syllable.

**The word is mitten.**
- **I tap 1 box for each syllable I hear: mit/ten.** (Place your hand under your chin while saying the syllables. Point out that your chin drops as you say each syllable.)
  - **There are 2 syllables.**

Day
**21**

- Now, I write the letters that represent the sounds in the first syllable.
  - The first syllable is mit.
    - First sound? /m/ Letter? m
    - Second sound? /ĭ/ Letter? i
    - Third sound? /t/ Letter? t
    - The syllable type and gesture are closed.
    - The syllable is mit.
- Now, I write the letters that represent the sounds in the second syllable.
  - The second syllable is ten.
    - First sound? /t/ Letter? t
    - Second sound? /ĕ/ Letter? e
    - Third sound? /n/ Letter? n
    - The syllable type and gesture are closed.
    - The syllable is ten.
- I slide a finger under each syllable, combining them and whisper "mitten."

Let's try the next word together. The word is <u>sunset</u>. Word? **sunset**
- I tap 1 box for each syllable we hear. **sun/set** How many syllables? **2**
- Now, I write the letters that represent the sounds in the syllables.
  - First syllable? **sun**
    - First sound? **/s/** Letter? **s**
    - Second sound? **/ŭ/** Letter? **u**
    - Third sound? **/n/** Letter? **n**
    - Syllable type and gesture? **closed**
    - Syllable? **sun**
  - Second syllable? **set**
    - First sound? **/s/** Letter? **s**
    - Second sound? **/ĕ/** Letter? **e**
    - Third sound? **/t/** Letter? **t**
    - Syllable type and gesture? **closed**
    - Syllable? **set**
- Word? **sunset**

Now it's your turn. Turn to page 38 in your Student Workbook. Here are the steps:

1. Say the word.
2. Tap a box for each syllable you hear.
3. For each syllable, say the sounds, write the letters, and say the syllable type while showing the gesture.
4. Slide your finger under both syllables and whisper read the word to yourself.

| mit | |
| --- | --- |

| mit | ten |
| --- | --- |

| | |
| --- | --- |

| sun | |
| --- | --- |

| sun | set |
| --- | --- |

*Note:* Remind students that they can finger-stretch sounds to spell the syllables.

## Answer Key

| Words to Dictate | Correct Answers in Student Workbook | |
|---|---|---|
| sunset | sun | set |
| 1. absent | ab | sent |
| 2. plastic | plas | tic |
| 3. contest | con | test |
| 4. problem | prob | lem |
| 5. rabbit | rab | bit |
| 6. unzip | un | zip |

## Passage Reading

### UNDERLINE PATTERN WORDS

### Passage – Literary: *The Rascal*

Now we'll practice finding multisyllable words with the closed-closed pattern in the passage. The passage today is about a rascal who is digging holes in the yard. Do you know what a rascal is? (a misbehaving or mischievous person or animal)

Today we are going to look for multisyllable words with the closed-closed pattern and underline them.

Let's look at the title of the passage. (Do not read the title.) **In the word** *Rascal*, **I see 2 vowel letters with 2 consonants between the vowels. The word** *Rascal* **is a multisyllable word with 2 closed syllables, so I underline it. Help me find more words to underline. Hold up the closed syllable gesture with both hands when you see another one, and I'll underline it.** (Continue underlining the closed-closed multisyllable words above the black line.)

**Now it's your turn. Turn to page 39 in your Student Workbook. Here are the steps:**

1. **Begin at the black line and continue to the end of the passage.**
2. **Use your fingers to find the vowels.**
3. **If you find a 2-syllable word with the closed-closed pattern, underline it.**

**I'll give you a few minutes and we'll check them together.**

Day
22

# DAY 22

## Phonological Awareness Warm-Up

Today we are going to practice <u>substituting, or changing, the vowel sound</u> in a word. Let's review the instructions:

- I'll say a word and you repeat it.
- Next, I'll tell you what sound to substitute, or change, in the word.
- Then, tell me the new word. Ready?

| | | | |
|---|---|---|---|
| Say sat: (**sat**) Change /ă/ to /ĭ/. Word? | **sit** | Say an: (**an**) Change /ă/ to /ŏ/. Word? | **on** |
| Say bet: (**bet**) Change /ĕ/ to /ă/. Word? | **bat** | Say and: (**and**) Change /ă/ to /ĕ/. Word? | **end** |
| Say bike: (**bike**) Change /ī/ to /ā/. Word? | **bake** | Say tin: (**tin**) Change /ĭ/ to /ĕ/. Word? | **ten** |
| Say desk: (**desk**) Change /ĕ/ to /ŭ/. Word? | **dusk** | Say dad: (**dad**) Change /ă/ to /ĭ/. Word? | **did** |
| Say fast: (**fast**) Change /ă/ to /ĭ/. Word? | **fist** | Say fun: (**fun**) Change /ŭ/ to /ă/. Word? | **fan** |
| Say big: (**big**) Change /ĭ/ to /ă/. Word? | **bag** | Say give: (**give**) Change /ĭ/ to /ā/. Word? | **gave** |
| Say trick: (**trick**) Change /ĭ/ to /ă/. Word? | **track** | Say made: (**made**) Change /ā/ to /ă/. Word? | **mad** |
| Say dump: (**dump**) Change /ŭ/ to /ă/. Word? | **damp** | Say run: (**run**) Change /ŭ/ to /ă/. Word? | **ran** |

## Phonics Pattern

### READING PATTERN WORDS

### Review the Pattern

We're continuing to practice reading and spelling multisyllable words with the closed-closed syllable pattern. Today we will add multisyllable words that follow 3 other syllable patterns: silent-e, vowel team, and vowel-r. Remember, every syllable must have a vowel sound.

Repeat after me: **Every syllable must have a vowel sound.**

Let's review the syllable types. I'll say the pattern and you say the syllable type and show the gesture.

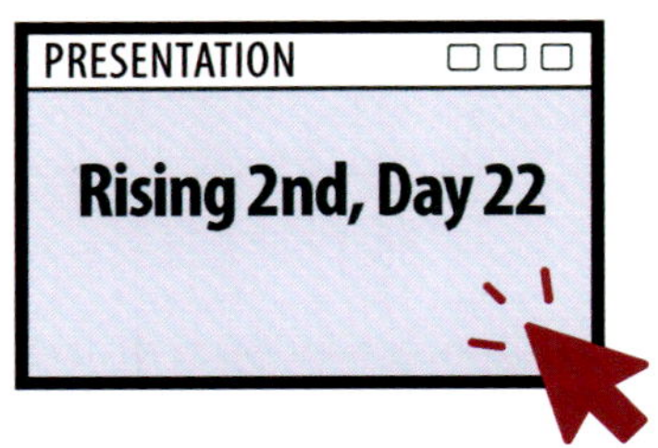


- Which syllable type has 1 vowel letter followed by 1 or more consonants?

 **closed**

- Which syllable type has 1 vowel letter, 1 consonant, and an e at the end?

 **silent-e**

- A vowel team syllable has 2 or more letters side by side that are pronounced as 1 vowel sound. The vowel team gesture is 2 fingers side by side. Practice it with me.

 **vowel team**

- A vowel-r syllable has 1 vowel followed by the consonant *r*. The vowel-r gesture is the middle finger crossed over the pointer finger. Practice it with me.

 **vowel-r**

Day **22**

## Read Pattern Words

Now, we're going to read multisyllable words with the closed, silent-e, vowel team, and vowel-r syllable patterns.

When I show you a word, follow these steps:
1. Find the vowels with both hands and say the number of vowel sounds.
2. Say the number of consonants between the vowels.
3. Say where we divide the syllables.
4. For each syllable, say the syllable type while showing the gesture, say the vowel sound, and read the syllable.
5. Read the word.

🔑 **Routine for Word Reading:**
- **Find the vowels.** (2 hands)
- **How many vowel sounds?**
- **How many consonants between the vowels?**
  – Where are the syllables divided?
- **For each syllable, ask:**
  – Syllable type and gesture?
  – Vowel sound?
  – Syllable?
- **Word?**

## Answer Key

| Word # | # of Vowel Sounds | # of Cons. Between the Vowels | Divide Between | First Syllable Type | First Syllable Sound | First Syllable Read | Second Syllable Type | Second Syllable Sound | Second Syllable Read | Word |
|---|---|---|---|---|---|---|---|---|---|---|
| 1. | 2 | 2 | n & d | closed | /ŭ/ | sun | closed | /ĕ/ | deck | sundeck |
| 2. | 2 | 2 | n & t | closed | /ĭ/ | win | vowel-r | /er/ | ter | winter |
| 3. | 2 | 2 | b & l | closed | /ŏ/ | prob | closed | /ĕ/ | lem | problem |
| 4. | 2 | 2 | r & f | vowel-r | /er/ | per | closed | /ĕ/ | fect | perfect |
| 5. | 2 | 2 | d & t | closed | /ĕ/ | bed | silent-e | /ī/ | time | bedtime |
| 6. | 2 | 2 | n & j | closed | /ĕ/ | en | vowel team | /oi/ | joy | enjoy |
| 7. | 2 | 2 | n & n | closed | /ĭ/ | din | vowel-r | /er/ | ner | dinner |
| 8. | 2 | 2 | m & s | closed | /ĭ/ | him | closed | /ĕ/ | self | himself |

**Note:** Although the words _bedtime_ and _enjoy_ have 3 vowels, there are only 2 vowel sounds.

## Phonics Pattern

### SORT SYLLABLES

Today, we will practice identifying, sorting, and reading the syllables in multisyllable words. The syllables follow the closed, silent-e, vowel team, and vowel-r syllable patterns. Let's do the first word together. (Students should be pointing and gesturing throughout the routine.)

(Display catnap.)
**Here is the word.** (Do not read the word.)

**Step 1: Find the vowels.**
- Use both hands to find the vowels in each syllable.
- Point to the first letter _a_ with the left pointer finger, and the other letter _a_ with the right point finger.
- **How many vowel sounds?** 2

**Step 2: Underline the vowels.**
- **Which letters should I underline to represent the vowel sounds?**
  **a and a**
- **This word has 2 vowel sounds.  How many syllables are there? 2**

ca<u>t</u>n<u>a</u>p

**Step 3: Draw a line between the syllables.**
- **How many consonants between the vowel sounds? 2**
- **Where do I draw a line? between the t and n**
- **I draw a syllable division line between the letters *t* and *n*.**

ca<u>t</u>|n<u>a</u>p

**Step 4: Read and sort each syllable.**

<table>
<tr><td>

**Sort the first syllable.**

**I cover the second syllable and look at the first one.**
- **Syllable type and gesture?**
  **closed**
- **Vowel sound? /ă/**
- **Syllable? cat**
- **Where do I write the syllable *cat*?**
  **closed syllable column**

</td><td>

**Sort the second syllable.**

**I cover the first syllable and look at the second one.**
- **Syllable type and gesture?**
  **closed**
- **Vowel sound? /ă/**
- **Syllable? nap**
- **Where do I write the syllable *nap*?**
  **closed syllable column**

</td></tr>
</table>

**Step 5: Read the word.**
- **Word? catnap**

| Divide Syllables | Closed | Silent-e | Vowel Team | Vowel-r |
|---|---|---|---|---|
| cat|nap | cat    nap | | | |

 **Now it's your turn. Turn to page 40 in your Student Workbook. Let's review the steps.**

1. **Find the vowels and underline them.**
2. **Count the consonants between the vowels. Remember, when there are 2 consonants between the vowels, divide between them.**
3. **Draw a line to divide the word.**
4. **Sort each syllable.**
   - **Say the syllable type and show the gesture.**
   - **Say the vowel sound and read the syllable.**
   - **Write the syllable in the correct column. Mark a V for silent-e, if there is one.**
5. **Read the word.**

**I'll check back with you in a few minutes and then you can check your answers.**

## Answer Key

| Divide Syllables | Closed | Silent-e | Vowel Team | Vowel-r |
|---|---|---|---|---|
| cat\|nap | cat    nap | | | |
| 1. sud\|den | sud    den | | | |
| 2. ad\|mit | ad    mit | | | |
| 3. per\|son | son | | | per |
| 4. ham\|mock | ham    mock | | | |
| 5. up\|date | up | date | | |
| 6. up\|per | up | | | per |
| 7. sun\|ray | sun | | ray | |
| 8. up\|hill | up    hill | | | |

**Note:** Guide students in sorting the syllables in #3, 4, and 7. The vowel team and vowel-r syllable types may still be challenging for students.

## Writing

### SYLLABLE MAPPING

**We've done syllable mapping before. Let's do one together.**

**The word is <u>public</u>. Word? public**

- **I tap 1 box for each syllable we hear. pub/lic How many syllables? 2**
- **Now, I write the letters that represent the sounds in the syllables.**
  - **First syllable? pub**
    - **First sound? /p/ Letter? p**
    - **Second sound? /ŭ/ Letter? u**
    - **Third sound? /b/ Letter? b**
    - **Syllable type and gesture? closed**
    - **Syllable? pub**
  - **Second syllable? lic**
    - **First sound? /l/ Letter? l**
    - **Second sound? /ĭ/ Letter? i**
    - **Third sound? /k/ Letter? c**
    - **Syllable type and gesture? closed**
    - **Syllable? lic**
- **Word? public**

**Now it's your turn. Turn to page 40 in your Student Workbook. Here are the steps:**

1. **Say the word.**
2. **Tap a box for each syllable you hear.**
3. **For each syllable, say the sounds, write the letters, and say the syllable type while showing the gesture.**
4. **Mark a V connecting the vowels if the syllable follows the silent-e pattern.**
5. **Slide your finger under both syllables and whisper read the word to yourself.**

| | |
|---|---|
| | |

| | |
|---|---|
| pub | |

| | |
|---|---|
| pub | lic |

**Note:** Remind students that they can finger-stretch sounds to spell the syllables.

## Answer Key

| Words to Dictate | Correct Answers in Student Workbook | |
|---|---|---|
| public | pub | lic |
| 1. gossip | gos | sip |
| 2. upset | up | set |
| 3. jigsaw | jig | saw |
| 4. after | af | ter |
| 5. inside | in | side |
| 6. kitten | kit | ten |

## Passage Reading

### READ PASSAGE

### Passage – Literary: *The Rascal*

Now we'll read the passage we underlined yesterday. This passage is about solving the mystery of who or what is making holes in the yard.

First, we'll read some of the underlined words together. When you see a 2-syllable word with the closed-closed syllable pattern, show me the closed gestures with both hands and read the word. What is the first underlined word? rascal Read with me just the underlined words above the black line.

Now it's your turn. Turn to page 39 in your Student Workbook. Here are the steps:

1.  First, whisper read all the underlined words in the rest of the passage.
2.  Then, go back to the beginning and whisper read the passage.

## Comprehension

### WRITTEN RESPONSE

In your Student Workbook, look at page 41. Complete the sentence from the passage. I'll give you a minute to do this, and then I'll ask for a couple of students to share what they wrote.

We used ____________ in the box to trap the ____________.
**(RL.1.1)**  (walnuts; rascal or chipmunk)

Day 23

# DAY 23

## Phonological Awareness Warm-Up

Today we are going to practice substituting, or changing, the vowel sound in a word. Let's review the instructions:

- I'll say a word and you repeat it.
- Next, I'll tell you what sound to substitute, or change, in the word.
- Then, tell me the new word. Ready?

| | | | | |
|---|---|---|---|---|
| Say had: (had) Change /ă/ to /ĕ/. Word? | head | Say pill: (pill) Change /ĭ/ to /ă/. Word? | pal |
| Say stick: (stick) Change /ĭ/ to /ă/. Word? | stack | Say tap: (tap) Change /ă/ to /ā/. Word? | tape |
| Say fill: (fill) Change /ĭ/ to /aw/. Word? | fall | Say hid: (hid) Change /ĭ/ to /ī/. Word? | hide |
| Say his: (his) Change /ĭ/ to /ă/. Word? | has | Say cop: (cop) Change /ŏ/ to /ō/. Word? | cope |
| Say bet: (bet) Change /ĕ/ to /ă/. Word? | bat | Say ate: (ate) Change /ā/ to /ă/. Word? | at |
| Say pin: (pin) Change /ĭ/ to /ă/. Word? | pan | Say fan: (fan) Change /ă/ to /ŭ/. Word? | fun |
| Say bit: (bit) Change /ĭ/ to /ă/. Word? | bat | Say net: (net) Change /ĕ/ to /ŭ/. Word? | nut |
| Say said: (said) Change /ĕ/ to /ă/. Word? | sad | Say bag: (bag) Change /ă/ to /ĭ/. Word? | big |

## Phonics Pattern

### WORD READING ACCURACY

Look at the words. These are all 2-syllable words that follow the closed, silent-e, vowel team, or vowel-r patterns. Let's read them together.

| | | | |
|---|---|---|---|
| attic | upset | after | hidden |
| sudden | bedtime | subject | enjoy |
| mitten | picnic | inside | unzip |
| tennis | dinner | kitten | yellow |
| problem | public | absent | object |

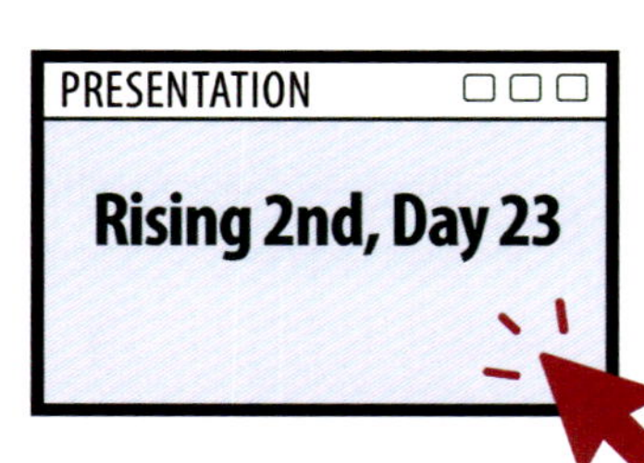

## Writing

### WORD BUILDING

Today we will use closed and long vowel silent-e syllables to build 2-syllable words. Syllables are word parts that have 1 vowel sound. Let's review the syllable types.

- **What is a closed syllable?** 1 vowel letter followed by 1 or more consonants, and the vowel sound is short
  - Gesture nd say the syllable type. closed
- **What is a long vowel silent-e syllable?** 1 vowel, 1 consonant, an e at the end, and the vowel sound is long
  - Gesture and say the syllable type. long vowel silent-e

Watch me do the first one. There are 2 lists—First Syllables and Second Syllables—to use when building multisyllable words.

- I begin by choosing a syllable from the First Syllables list. I write the syllable *nap* on the first line.

$$\underline{nap} + \underline{\ \ } = \underline{\ \ }$$

- Next, I try other syllables from the Second Syllables list to combine with my first syllable until I build a word I know.
  - nap-hill. That isn't a word.
  - nap-tub. Again, that's not a word I know.
  - nap-kin. Yes, that makes a word I know.
- I write the syllable *kin* after the plus sign.

$$\underline{nap} + \underline{kin} = \underline{\ \ }$$

- Next, I write the word *napkin* on the line after the equal sign.
- Finally, I slide my finger under the word and whisper "napkin."

$$\underline{nap} + \underline{kin} = \underline{napkin}$$

| First Syllables | |
|---|---|
| nap | bath |
| up | back |
| in | sun |
| fit | hot |
| chip | pic |

| Second Syllables | |
|---|---|
| hill | side |
| tub | munk |
| kin | nic |
| ness | set |
| dog | pack |

**Turn to page 41 in your Student Workbook. Now you're going to build 2-syllable words. Let's review the steps.**

1. **Read all the syllables in both lists.**
2. **Choose a syllable from the First Syllables list and write it on the first line.**
3. **Choose a syllable from the Second Syllables list and blend it with the first syllable to see if it makes a word you know. If not, try another combination of syllables until you make a known word.**
4. **When you build a word you know, write the syllable on the second line after the plus sign.**
5. **Put both syllables together to make a new multisyllable word and write it on the third line after the equal sign.**
6. **Read the word to check your work.**
7. **Continue until you have built 4 multisyllable words you recognize. You may use syllables from each column more than once.**

**Answer Key**

| Multisyllable Words | |
|---|---|
| nap + kin | napkin |
| chip + munk | chipmunk |
| up + set | upset |
| fit + ness | fitness |
| in + side | inside |
| pic + nic | picnic |
| bath + tub | bathtub |
| up + hill | uphill |
| hot + dog | hotdog |
| back + pack | backpack |
| sun + set | sunset |

**Note:** As a strategy for adding engagement, or to scaffold this activity, you can have groups or pairs of students put these syllables on index cards or sticky notes. Students can collaborate while manipulating the syllables to build words.

## Passage Reading

## UNDERLINE PATTERN WORDS

### Passage – Informational: *Sundecks*

**Now it's time to practice with a new passage. This passage is about sundecks. Has anyone been on a sundeck on a ship, a boat, or the back of a house?**

**We'll underline multisyllable words with the 4 syllable patterns: closed, silent-e, vowel team, and vowel-r. Let's begin with the title. Which is the first word to underline?** sundecks

**Note:** To help students focus on visually identifying multisyllable words, use the "thumbs up" gesture versus using the 4 different syllable gestures for this activity.

**Help me find more multisyllable words. If you see a multisyllable word, show me a "thumbs up" with both hands and I'll underline it.** (Continue underlining the 2-syllable words to the black line.)

 **Now it's your turn. Turn to page 42 in your Student Workbook. Let's review the steps.**

1. **Begin below the black line and continue to the end of the passage.**
2. **Look at each word and point to the vowels.**
3. **If the word has 2 syllables, draw a line under it.**

**I'll give you a few minutes and we'll check them together.**

# DAY 24

## Phonological Awareness Warm-Up

**Today we are going to practice substituting, or changing, the vowel sound in a word. Let's review the instructions:**
- **I'll say a word and you repeat it.**
- **Next, I'll tell you what sound to substitute, or change, in the word.**
- **Then, tell me the new word. Ready?**

| | | | |
|---|---|---|---|
| Say can: (**can**) Change /ă/ to /ā/. Word? | **cane** | Say cup: (**cup**) Change /ŭ/ to /ŏ/. Word? | **cop** |
| Say beat: (**beat**) Change /ē/ to /ă/. Word? | **bat** | Say my: (**my**) Change /ī/ to /ā/. Word? | **may** |
| Say spice: (**spice**) Change /ī/ to /ā/. Word? | **space** | Say pick: (**pick**) Change /ĭ/ to /ă/. Word? | **pack** |
| Say deck: (**deck**) Change /ĕ/ to /ŭ/. Word? | **duck** | Say slip: (**slip**) Change /ĭ/ to /ă/. Word? | **slap** |
| Say than: (**than**) Change /ă/ to /ĕ/. Word? | **then** | Say lip: (**lip**) Change /ĭ/ to /ă/. Word? | **lap** |
| Say had: (**had**) Change /ă/ to /ĭ/. Word? | **hid** | Say pot: (**pot**) Change /ŏ/ to /ĕ/. Word? | **pet** |
| Say get: (**get**) Change /ĕ/ to /ŭ/. Word? | **gut** | Say clap: (**clap**) Change /ă/ to /ĭ/. Word? | **clip** |
| Say cat: (**cat**) Change /ă/ to /ŭ/. Word? | **cut** | Say rock: (**rock**) Change /ŏ/ to /ă/. Word? | **rack** |

## Fluency

### HIGH-FREQUENCY WORDS

Display the high-frequency word grid. Prompt students by saying **"Word?"** at each box.

| | | | |
|---|---|---|---|
| have | live | once | round |
| give | open | thank | put |
| said | how | please | find |
| pretty | too | well | know |

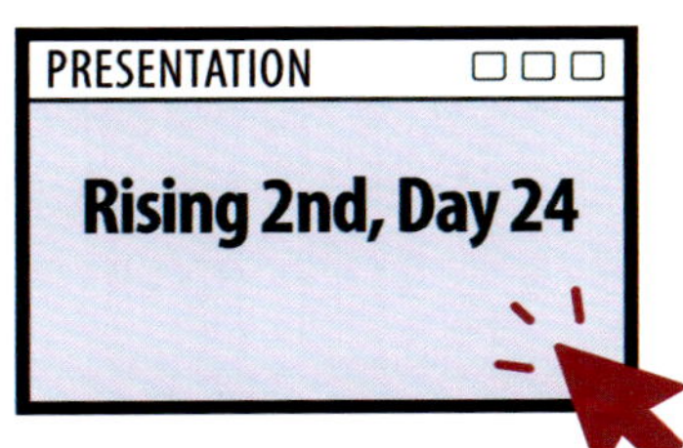


 

**Day 24**

 **Now it's your turn. Turn to page 43 in your Student Workbook. When I say "begin," tap under the first word and whisper it. Read across the rows until I say "stop." Circle the last word you read. If you finish before I say "stop," go up to the top and read the words again.** (Time students for 1 minute. Say "stop" and ask students to circle the last word that was read.)

| | | | |
|---|---|---|---|
| too | thank | put | said |
| have | how | know | once |
| give | round | please | open |
| again | pretty | live | well |

## Writing

### WORD CHAINS

It's word chain time! We've done this on other days but today we'll change a syllable in each 2-syllable word rather than a sound. We'll change 1 syllable at a time to spell a new word.

Let's do the first one together.

The first word is <u>unkind</u>.

Let's change <u>unkind</u> to <u>until</u>.
  • Which syllable changes? the syllable *kind* changes to *til*
  • How do we spell the new word? u-n-t-i-l
I write the word *until* under *unkind*.

Next, I change <u>until</u> to <u>unwell</u>.
  • Which syllable changes? the syllable *til* changes to *well*
  • How do we spell the new word? u-n-w-e-l-l
I write the word *unwell* under *until*.

Finally, I change <u>unwell</u> to <u>unpack</u>.
  • Which syllable changes? the syllable *well* changes to *pack*
  • How do we spell the new word? u-n-p-a-c-k
I write the word *unpack* under *unwell*.

**Now it's your turn. Turn to page 43 in your Student Workbook. You'll find a spot to write 4 word chains. I'll tell you 1 word at a time and you'll write each new word below the old one. Find the page and look up when you're ready.**

| |
|---|
| unkind |
| until |
| unwell |
| unpack |

***Note:*** If you are writing the words on the board, make sure you build the words going down, not across.

**Routine for Word Chains:**
• Change word *x* to word *y*.
  – Which syllable changes?
  – How do we spell the new word?
• Write word *y* under word *x*.

## Answer Key

| | | | |
|---|---|---|---|
| unzip | disrupt | uphill | into |
| uncap | dismiss | uplift | insult |
| unclip | discuss | upheld | invent |
| unroll | discard | upset | indent |

## Passage Reading

### READ PASSAGE

### Passage – Informational: *Sundecks*

Now it's time to read a passage. This passage is about sundecks.

First, we'll read some of the underlined words together. When you see an underlined multisyllable word, read it with me. What is the underlined word in the title? sundecks Read with me just the underlined words above the black line.

Now it's your turn. Turn to page 42 in your Student Workbook. Let's review the steps.

1.  First, whisper read all the underlined words in the rest of the passage.
2.  Then, go back to the beginning and whisper read the story.

## Comprehension

### ORAL RESPONSE

Now that you've read the passage, let's talk about it.
*   **What is a sundeck? (RI.1.1)** (a sitting area in the sun)
*   **Where can you find sundecks? (RI.1.1)** (a ship, a small boat, at home)

Day
**25**

# DAY 25

## Phonological Awareness Warm-Up

**Today we are going to practice substituting, or changing, the vowel sound in a word. Let's review the instructions:**
- **I'll say a word and you repeat it.**
- **Next, I'll tell you what sound to substitute, or change, in the word.**
- **Then, tell me the new word. Ready?**

| | | | | |
|---|---|---|---|
| Say tell: (**tell**) Change /ĕ/ to /ĭ/. Word? | **till** | Say wash: (**wash**) Change /aw/ to /ĭ/. Word? | **wish** |
| Say it: (**it**) Change /ĭ/ to /ă/. Word? | **at** | Say book: (**book**) Change /oo/ to /ă/. Word? | **back** |
| Say try: (**try**) Change /ī/ to /ā/. Word? | **tray** | Say shout: (**shout**) Change /ou/ to /ē/. Word? | **sheet** |
| Say is: (**is**) Change /ĭ/ to /ă/. Word? | **as** | Say math: (**math**) Change /ă/ to /ŏ/. Word? | **moth** |
| Say crash: (**crash**) Change /ă/ to /ŭ/. Word? | **crush** | Say back: (**back**) Change /ă/ to /ī/. Word? | **bike** |
| Say spin: (**spin**) Change /ĭ/ to /ī/. Word? | **spine** | Say fin: (**fin**) Change /ĭ/ to /ī/. Word? | **fine** |
| Say dash: (**dash**) Change /ă/ to /ĭ/. Word? | **dish** | Say kit: (**kit**) Change /ĭ/ to /ī/. Word? | **kite** |
| Say rush: (**rush**) Change /ŭ/ to /ă/. Word? | **rash** | Say which: (**which**) Change /ĭ/ to /ŏ/. Word? | **watch** |

## Fluency

### SORT SYLLABLES

**Today, we will practice identifying, sorting, and reading the syllables in multisyllable words. The syllables follow the closed and silent-e syllable patterns. Let's do the first word together.** (Students should be pointing and gesturing throughout the routine.)

(Display <u>zigzag</u>.)

**Here is the word.** (Do not read the word.)

<u>Step 1</u>: **Find the vowels.**
- **Use both hands to find the vowels in each syllable.**
- **Point to the letter *i* with the left pointer finger and the letter *a* with the right pointer finger.**
- **How many vowel sounds?** **2**

<u>Step 2</u>: **Underline the vowels.**
- **Which letters do I underline to represent the vowel sounds?** **i and a**
- **This word has 2 vowel sounds. How many syllables?** **2**

<u>Step 3</u>: **Draw a line between the syllables.**
- **How many consonants between the vowel sounds?** **2**
- **Where do I draw the line?** **between and the g and z**
- **I draw a syllable division line between the letters *g* and *z*.**

PRESENTATION ☐☐☐

**Rising 2nd, Day 25**

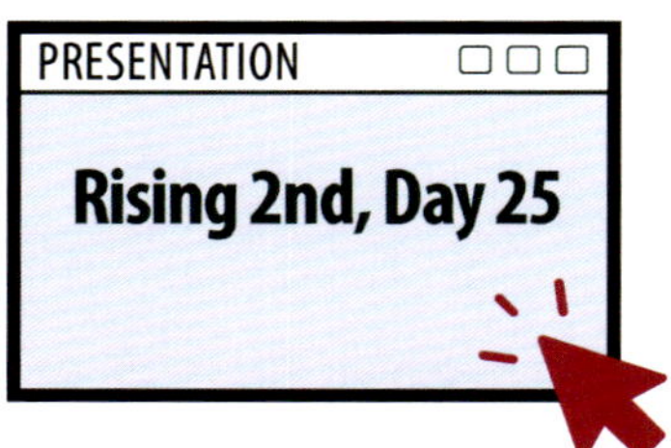

zigzag

zigzag

zig|zag

 95 Phonics Booster Bundle™: Summer School Edition 2021 • Rising Second • Teacher's Edition

**Let's do the next step together.**

**Step 4: Read each syllable.**

| | |
|---|---|
| **Sort the first syllable.**  <br> **Cover the second syllable and look at the first one.** <br> • Syllable type? closed <br> • Vowel sound? /ĭ/ <br> • Syllable? zig <br> • Where do I write the syllable *zig*? <br>   closed syllable column | **Sort the second syllable.** <br> **Cover the first syllable and look at the second one.** <br> • Syllable type? closed <br> • Vowel sound? /ă/ <br> • Syllable? zag <br> • Where do I write the syllable *zag*? <br>   closed syllable column |

**Step 5: Read the word.**
- **Word?** zigzag

| Divide Syllables | Closed | Silent-e |
|---|---|---|
| zig\|zag | zig    zag | |

 **Now it's your turn. Turn to page 44 in your Student Workbook. Here are the steps:**

1. **Find the vowels and underline them.**
2. **Count the consonants between the vowels. Remember, when there are 2 consonants between the vowel sounds, divide between them.**
3. **Draw a line to divide the word.**
4. **For each syllable:**
   - **Whisper the syllable type while showing the gesture.**
   - **Whisper the vowel sound.**
   - **Write the syllable in the correct column. Mark a V for silent-e, if there is one.**
   - **Whisper read the syllable.**
5. **Read the word.**

**Answer Key**

| Divide Syllables | Closed | Silent-e |
|---|---|---|
| zig\|zag | zig    zag | |
| 1. him\|self | him    self | |
| 2. un\|made | un | made |
| 3. sun\|lamp | sun    lamp | |
| 4. mis\|take | mis | take |
| 5. gos\|sip | gos    sip | |

Day
**25**

## Fluency

### SENTENCES

We will practice reading words with 2 syllables in sentences.

Look at this sentence grid. Please read it aloud chorally as a class. Ready?

| He made a mistake. | The kitten is under the mat. | Please open the window. |

**Now it's your turn. Turn to page 44 in your Student Workbook. When I say "begin," point to the first sentence and whisper it. Continue reading across the page. If you finish before I say "stop," start at the top and read the sentences again.** (Time students for 1 minute. Say "stop" and ask students to circle the last sentence that was read.)

| Please unzip the tent. | It is bedtime. | Play inside until dinner. |
|---|---|---|
| He made a mistake. | She will take a catnap. | Go to sleep after the show. |
| The kitten is under the mat. | Enter the contest. | Please open the window. |
| I will go to the dentist. | Eat some dinner. | I hope you enjoy the song. |

## Writing

### SENTENCE WRITING

**On page 45 of your Student Workbook, there are some lines to write sentences. Today you will write 2 sentences using the** words from the Word Bank on the bottom of page 44. Use at least 2 words from the Word Bank in each sentence.

| Word Bank | | | |
|---|---|---|---|
| inside | picnic | after | bedtime |
| enjoy | subject | unzip | dinner |
| upset | problem | mistake | rabbit |

(answers vary: Check for complete sentences and correct use of words from the Word Bank.)

## Passage Reading

### READ PASSAGES

Today you are going to practice reading both of the passages. One was about a rascal who digs holes. The second was about sundecks.

## Comprehension

### WRITTEN RESPONSE

Turn to page 45 in your Student Workbook. Read both passages, then write the answers to the 2 questions for each passage in your workbook.

**Passage – Literary:** *The Rascal* on page 39
1. **Who did they think was the rascal at first? (RL.1.1)** (the hound, Bandit)
2. **What was digging holes in the yard? (RL.1.1)** (a chipmunk)

**Passage – Informational:** *Sundecks* on page 42
1. **What can you lay on when on a sundeck? (RI.1.4)** (a chair or hammock)
2. **What can you do if the sundeck is old and dark? (RI.1.1)** (update it with pastel paint or fresh stain)